Seen But Not Heard

Co-ordinating Community
Child Health and Social Services
for Children in Need

Detailed Evidence and
Guidelines for Managers and
Practitioners

LONDON: HMSO

Printed in the UK for the Audit Commission at Press on Printers, London
Photographs by Hilary Shedel, and Format Partners
Cover Photograph: with thanks to Hector and Hester

ISBN 011 886 113 1

Preface

The Audit Commission oversees the external audit of local authorities and agencies within the National Health Service (NHS) in England and Wales. As part of this function the Commission is charged with reviewing the economy, efficiency and effectiveness of services provided by these bodies. To this end, studies and audits of selected topics are undertaken each year.

The study of children's services which forms the subject of this report breaks new ground in that it looks across the agency boundaries between community child health and social services. New legislation has changed the framework within which these services operate. The report reviews the problems this poses for the agencies concerned, and the actions they are taking to change from traditional patterns of working to a much closer collaboration which focuses on the individual requirements of families and children in need of support.

Not all services are covered in the report. The study provides an overview of child health surveillance, the school health service, immunisation, family support and daycare, child protection and children looked after by social services. The needs of children with disabilities are highlighted.

Under the directorship of Dr Ross Tristem, assisted by David Browning, the project was undertaken by Claire Blackman and Beverley Fitzsimons. Jonathan Sercombe and John Russell assisted in the preparation and analysis of data. Full-time assistance was given by Colin Bott, Social Services Inspectorate, Department of Health and Jean Georgeson, former director of community nursing. Consultants to the team were Rob Sykes, Director of Operations, Oxfordshire social services and Anthony Harrison.

Table of Contents

SUMMARY   1

INTRODUCTION   5
— Background   5
— The key themes   7
— Structure of the report   8

1. THE WELL-BEING OF THE CHILD   9
— A child's perspective   9
— Implications for service delivery   12
— Spending and service patterns   13

2. THE SERVICE RESPONSE – PROBLEMS IDENTIFIED   17
— Joint activities   17
    Formulating strategy   17
    Operational areas of common interest   20
— Community child health: surveillance, immunisation and school health   29
    surveillance and immunisation   29
    School health   31
— Social services: social work and children looked after   32
    Social work   32
    Children 'looked after'   33
— Summary of problems   35

3. MOVING FORWARD   37
— Developing joint partnerships   37
    Joint assessment of needs and development of a strategy   37
— Operational areas of common interest   38
— An agenda for health commissioners   47
    Surveillance and immunisation   48
    Child health clinics   48
    School health   50
    Monitoring and evaluation   51
— An agenda for providers of community child health   52
    What are the health needs of the population?   52
    What priorities and criteria are being adopted?   53

Reviewing services and costs 57

Reviewing field social work practice and organisation 57

Reviewing residential care 58

Setting a new course in social services 59

Improving information systems 60

Field social work 61

Children looked after 64

4. SUMMARY OF RECOMMENDATIONS 71

— Developing joint partnerships 71

Joint assessment of needs and development of a strategy 71

Operational areas of common interest 71

— An agenda for health commissioners 72

Surveillance and immunisation 72

Child health clinics 72

GP Fundholders 73

School health 73

Monitoring and evaluation 73

— An agenda for providers of community child health 73

What are the health needs of the population? 73

What priorities and criteria are being adopted? 73

What skills are required? 73

What information is required? 73

How should the service be organised? 73

— An agenda for social services for children 74

Reviewing services and costs 74

Reviewing field social work practice and organisation 74

Reviewing residential care 74

— Setting a new course in social services 74

Improving information systems 74

Field social work 74

Children looked after 74

APPENDIX 1 77

APPENDIX 2 79

GLOSSARY OF TERMS 81

REFERENCES 85

INDEX 89

Summary

Children, because of their vulnerability, must be supported and protected by others. The primary responsibility for this rests with their parents, but the state also has responsibilities to ensure help is provided. Some is universally available to all children, such as education, care when they are sick, or checks to ensure they are developing normally (child health surveillance). Family support, however, may be provided on a selective basis depending on need (Exhibit 1).

A number of health and social factors can adversely affect children, causing them to be in need. These include, a poor environment, poverty, family stress, lack of good parenting, mental and physical ill health and disability. As a result, their health or development can cause concern. Problems with behaviour and delinquency can occur. In extreme cases they may be neglected or abused and may need protection. If their families can no longer look after them, they may need to be looked after in foster or residential care.

Support is provided by primary and community health services, local authorities and voluntary bodies among others. The degree of support will vary, depending on the needs of families and children.

Recently, the framework for providing some of this support has been extensively recast. *The National Health Service and Community Care Act 1990* (Ref. 1) has introduced a separation between the commissioning of services and their provision. The *1990 GP contract* (Ref. 2) and the introduction of GP fundholding have increased the involvement of GPs in community child health services such as surveillance. And *The Children Act 1989* (Ref. 3) has required social services authorities to take responsibility for identifying and supporting 'children in need'.

Exhibit 1
SUPPORT OFFERED BY HEALTH AND SOCIAL SERVICES
Family support may be provided depending on need

Needs (illustrative only)

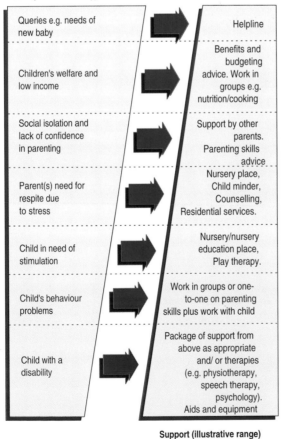

Support (illustrative range)

Source: Audit Commission

The changes demanded by the new legislation require major adjustments to the way agencies discharge these responsibilities and relate to each other. Traditionally, the health service has provided services universally available to all, while local authority social services have provided more highly targeted support. Although this broad distinction remains, in future community health agencies will need to focus more of their scarce resources, while local authorities will need to broaden their remit to promote a wider range of initiatives that provide families with support. As a result, many activities fall within the remit of both; and even areas exclusive to the NHS are shared between GPs and community child health services. The potential for duplication, confusion and waste is considerable unless these changes are managed effectively. Many authorities are aware of the challenges they face and are taking steps to address them.

Community health and social services spend £2 billion per year on these services. If they are to be provided in the most cost effective way and fulfil the requirements of the Children Act, authorities must:

— focus on the needs of children and families and provide services which meet specific objectives

— check outcomes to verify effectiveness of services

— work jointly to provide an integrated range of services and work in partnership with parents.

To translate these key areas into action requires initiatives at every level. **Central Government** should promote inter-agency co-ordination by raising the status of children's services plans which should be joint and mandatory, and which should be published (making them equivalent to community care plans). **Joint action** between health, social services and education authorities is needed to formulate these plans, which should contain joint assessment of needs, agreements on the needs to be addressed, the extent of those needs and their relative priorities. The plans should also focus on:

— family support, identifying each agency's role and jointly-funding initiatives such as Homestart and Newpin which encourage parents to help other parents

— child protection arrangements, ensuring that each agency's role is clear

— children with disabilities, providing a higher profile within a common framework

— children looked after, ensuring access to education and health care, and to support on leaving care

There should also be action within each agency. **Health commissioners** should start to shape and direct health services for children more effectively, determining needs, targeting services and evaluating outcomes within a clear purchasing plan:

— needs should be assessed and prioritised for action

— immunisation and child health surveillance programmes should follow national guidelines

— after a universally-provided first visit for families with new babies, health visiting should be focused on families with identified needs; written guidance and help lines should be provided for new parents

— community child health clinics should be commissioned selectively to avoid unnecessary duplication and waste

— local projects - often in conjunction with voluntary and private groups addressing assessed needs -should be promoted and evaluated

— the school health service's purpose should be defined more precisely, with a re-assessment of the relative roles of school nurses and school medical officers

— information requirements should be identified which allow the effectiveness of services commissioned and progress with the contract to be monitored.

Providers of children's community health services must be able to justify their activities to health commissioners within the overall children's services plan. They should:

— target agreed needs, using information from practitioners

— evaluate services effectively

— adjust the skill-mix to match the workload

— improve information systems

— review how best to deploy staff - by patch, GP practice or a mixture of the two.

Social services departments must develop a more proactive rather than reactive approach, paying particular attention to Part III section 17 of the Children Act which covers authorities' responsibilities to children in need. They should:

— identify where children in need are living and allocate resources accordingly

— review existing services, their costs and effectiveness in relation to needs, releasing resources for re deployment wherever possible

— review social work practice and organisation, focusing on
    — effective workload management and supervision

    — time management

    — referral procedures and specialisations

    — the implementation of a needs-led rather than a service-driven approach

— develop clear strategies that strike a balance between needs and resources and encourage the growth of proactive support services

— improve information systems in order to be able to link needs, services and outcomes in a demonstrable way

— develop clear, timetabled plans to implement strategies and produce a well managed service.

Because of the scale and complexity of the topic, it has been necessary to circumscribe the study: adoption services, services for children with mental health problems, and for children and young people in trouble with the law have all been excluded. In due course they may be the subject of future studies in their own right since the Commission acknowledges their importance to the well-being of the child. In addition, the key role of voluntary sector organisations has not been examined in detail. The report does not address services to children who are sick (which was the subject of a separate report). And although a review of education provision did not form part of this review, it is clear that help with parenting skills is required by a number of families in close contact with health and social services. Serious consideration should be given to including the teaching of such skills within the school curriculum.

Adjustments to health and social services should be made within the overall framework of the agreed children's services plan. In this way the common themes of measuring and identifying need, focusing services accordingly and improving the evaluation of the resulting impact should lead to improvements in support given to some of the most vulnerable children in our society. Health commissioners, providers and social services must recognise resource and time implications associated with adopting the approach advocated in this report and ensure they are made available. This extra investment should lead to significant gains in efficiency and effectiveness that more than compensate.

Introduction

BACKGROUND

1. Children aged under 18 make up nearly a quarter of the population but because of their immaturity they have no voice in matters to do with their well-being. The prime responsibility for this rests with their parents. But the state has a supporting role ensuring that essential services are available to all children and families, protecting those children whose parents abuse or neglect them, and, as a last resort, sharing in parental responsibility.

2. The responsibilities of parents and the state are extensive. The *United Nations (UN) Convention on the Rights of the Child* (Ref. 4), to which the government has agreed, lists the main areas of economic, social and health care (Exhibit 2).

Exhibit 2

THE UNITED NATIONS CONVENTION ON THE RIGHTS OF THE CHILD.

Nine main areas are listed in economic, social and health care

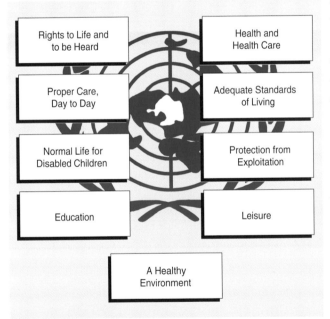

Rights to Life and to be Heard	Health and Health Care
Proper Care, Day to Day	Adequate Standards of Living
Normal Life for Disabled Children	Protection from Exploitation
Education	Leisure
A Healthy Environment	

Source: Guide to the UN Convention

3. Although the Government has, with some exclusions, ratified the Convention there is no single statement in which it sets out its responsibilities across all the relevant areas. *The Children Act 1989* (Ref. 3) comes closest, although it covers directly only a small part of the wider responsibilities of the Convention. It does, nevertheless, impose a general duty on local authorities to safeguard and promote the welfare of children in need – defined as those who are disabled, or for whom a 'reasonable standard' of health or development is at risk in various ways without the provision of services. The Act also recognises, explicitly, that services must be provided in partnership with parents.

4. Neither the Children Act nor the UN Convention contains precise targets or defines the levels of service required. The Act states that children in need are those unlikely to achieve or maintain a 'reasonable standard' of health or development unless services are provided. But 'reasonable standard' is not defined and neither are the indicators which would suggest such a standard is not being met.

5. Responsibilities are fragmented across a wide range of agencies. In the case of the Children Act, local authorities are urged to ensure that education and social services work

together and that both combine properly with health services. But the Act does not provide any specific machinery to ensure that services co-ordinate, nor (except for reviews of services for children aged under eight) does it set any specific requirements for them to do so.

6. Despite the importance of a child's health for morbidity in later life, only four targets for health improvements for children have been set in England. These concern accidents, smoking, teenage pregnancies - all within the framework of the *Health of the Nation* initiative (Ref. 5) - and immunisation, for which the National Health Service Management Executive has set national targets for all health authorities. In Wales, the Welsh Office and NHS Directorate have issued a *Protocol for Investment in Health Gain* (Ref. 6) which includes a separate section on *Maternal and Early Child Health*. Targets cover both service delivery and health gains.

7. Responsibility for immunisation lies clearly with the NHS, but any policy for reducing accidents, for example, requires contributions from a wide range of public agencies. The same is true in many other areas e.g. support for parents. Furthermore, the physical, emotional, social and psychological well-being of children are affected by a wide range of services - for example transport, health, housing, environmental protection, as well as national policies for income support, child benefit and so on.

8. The framework for state intervention has been extensively recast by recent legislative and contractual changes. The *NHS and Community Care Act 1990* has separated the commissioning of services from their provision, particularly in the health service, changing the emphasis from the provision of services to the meeting of needs. The *Children Act 1989* has consolidated much previous child care legislation, rebalancing the relationship between families and the state; and it has introduced a new responsibility for social services authorities to identify children in need and provide pro-active support. The Act empowers social services to ask other agencies to help provide these services, although, unlike community care, jointly-produced plans for children's services are recommended rather than mandatory. Within the NHS, the *1990 GP contract* has introduced additional incentives for GPs to become more involved with health promotion, child health surveillance, and the immunisation of children - also the province of the community child health services; and the introduction of GP fundholding has meant that some community child health services are commissioned directly by GPs rather than by district health authorities.

9. All of these changes require major adjustments to the way agencies discharge their responsibilities and relate to each other. Traditionally, the health service has provided universally available services, while local authority social services have provided more highly targeted support. Although this broad distinction remains, in future, health agencies will need to focus more of their scarce resources, while local authorities will need to broaden their remit to promote a wider range of initiatives that provide families with support. As a result, many activities fall within the remit of both the NHS and local authorities and even areas exclusive to the NHS are shared between GPs and community child health services. The potential for duplication, confusion and waste is considerable unless these changes are managed effectively.

THE KEY THEMES

10. To fulfil the expectations of the *Children Act* and the *NHS and Community Care Act*, and provide the most cost-effective support to children in need the following key requirements must be met.

— **Services must respond to and be focused on need.**

The *Children Act* requires authorities to identify 'children in need'. In areas such as education and primary preventive health care, the main task is to ensure worthwhile and well-organised universal provision and encourage universal uptake. In others, such as child protection, the task is to identify and provide services on a selective basis. In the latter case, failure to target means not only a waste of resources but also a failure to ensure the well-being of those children who slip through the net of universal services, or for whom universal provision is insufficient.

— **Services should only be offered where there is a likelihood of beneficial outcomes for the child and the family. (It may include the prevention of deterioration and intermediate outcomes as well as positive improvements in long term well-being.)**

This general principle is self-evident but at the same time difficult to apply. As chapter two demonstrates, there is little readily available information about how resources are currently being consumed and still less on how effectively they are being used. Inappropriate interventions are not only wasteful, they can also be detrimental to both child and parents.

— **The provision of services must jointly be co-ordinated and based on a partnership between agencies and parents.**

Because of the range of services which bear on the well-being of children, it is inevitable that a large number of agencies will be involved in providing them. There is a risk both of overlap or duplication on the one hand and, on the other, of services not being provided at all. This is particularly so where expenditure is incurred by one agency but the benefits, in terms of reduction in treatment costs, accrue to another, or where benefits may be long-term and agencies may be paying more attention to short-term outcomes. And as the *Children Act* recognises, the relationship between parents and the state should be one of partnership. The terms of that partnership will vary from service to service. In some, it is a matter of providing universal services. In others, it will involve supporting a minority of parents in the roles that the majority can take on for themselves.

* * *

11. Health and social services spend about £2 billion on the services covered by this report. In order to ensure that these very considerable resources are used to best effect, the Audit Commission has undertaken a study of current arrangements and how they are changing; and local auditors appointed by the Commission are reviewing arrangements in each health and local authority. The Commission is in an ideal position to help, as it appoints auditors to both health and local authorities. Because of the scale and complexity of the topic, it has been necessary to circumscribe the study. Immunisation, child health surveillance, school health services, family support, child protection and children looked after by social services departments form the subjects of the report. Children with a disability are highlighted. Child mental health and the youth justice service have not been covered as they are significant subjects in their own right – their importance to the well-being of the child is acknowledged by the Commission. In addition, the key role of voluntary sector organisations has not been examined in detail. Hospital services for children who are sick have been covered in an earlier Audit Commission report (Ref. 7) and the provision of education for children with special needs was the subject of investigation in *Getting in on the Act* (Ref. 8). During the course of the study, services in eight local authorities were and eight health authorities reviewed comprehensively. Particular services were examined in some detail in many other authorities.

STRUCTURE OF THE REPORT

12. The report is structured into four chapters.

Chapter one considers some of the influences which can have an adverse affect on a child's well-being, so creating a need for support from health and social services. It then outlines responses made, and the spending and service patterns of these agencies.

Chapter two reviews the problems identified, drawing on evidence from research, visits to eight health and eight social services authorities and surveys conducted by the Commission. The services are reviewed against the key themes outlined above.

Chapter three outlines, agency by agency, the way forward for health and social services if they are to improve the provision of services.

Chapter Four summarises the recommendations.

1. The Well-being of the Child

A CHILD'S PERSPECTIVE

13. Children may flourish, in terms of their physical and mental development and in their own sense of well-being, in a wide range of circumstances. Equally, threats to their well-being may come from a wide range of interacting and sometimes mutually reinforcing sources. Some children are born with disabilities which mean that they are unlikely to participate in the same activities as their peers without special support. Some are more prone to ill health and need greater care from health professionals. Some are brought up in physical circumstances which threaten their health. Some do not experience the degree of parental care that they need to flourish.

14. The volume of research bearing on the factors determining the well-being of children is too vast to summarise here. A study by the King's Fund Institute (Ref. 9) illustrates the range and nature of the factors at work. The links between these factors are complex. For simplicity of presentation, they have been grouped into the following categories: personal circumstances, parents' material circumstances, family structure, and environmental factors (Exhibit 3). However, the precise nature of the links is hard to demonstrate and objective measures of a lack of well-being and of ill-health are rare. Overall, however, there is little doubt that these factors have a critical influence on whether children do or do not flourish. They are considered in turn below.

Exhibit 3
CHILDREN'S WELL-BEING
Threats to their well-being come from a wide range of interacting and sometimes mutually re-enforcing sources

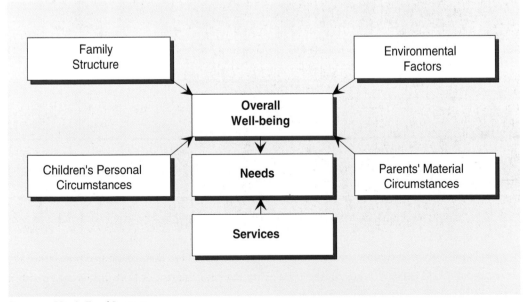

Source: King's Fund Institute

9

15. **Children's Personal Circumstances:** some determinants of the well being of children are genetic, such as inherited medical conditions. Some of these conditions are more common than others but most show little correlation with social or economic circumstances. In addition to the child's physical inheritance, their own behaviour - smoking, choice of food, exercise - and their educational experience also have an impact (Ref. 10).

16. **Parents' Material Circumstances:** a large number of studies show that material circumstances are closely related to the well-being of the child. Families in poor material circumstances are more likely than average to have children who die in childhood or suffer ill-health. Furthermore, there is a clear link between social class - a rough proxy for income - and mortality from accidents (Exhibit 4). A recent publication: *Children, Teenagers and Health* (Ref. 10) has brought together relevant data on non-medical influences on a child's well-being. In children up to the age of 15 rates of death, illness, accidents and behaviour problems all show differences by social class, indicating that inequalities in child health still exist.

Exhibit 4
PARENTS' MATERIAL CIRCUMSTANCES
Material circumstances are closely related to child well-being

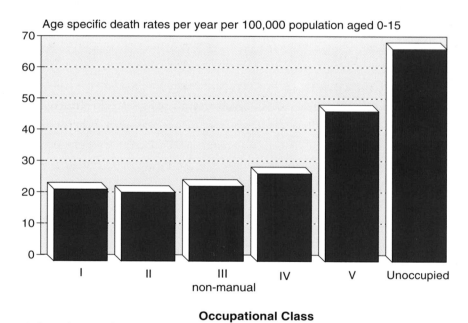

Age specific death rates per year per 100,000 population aged 0-15

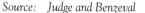

Occupational Class

Source: *Judge and Benzeval*

17. **Family Structure:** Children of parents who divorce are more likely to suffer from behavioural problems and ill-health (Ref. 10) and infant mortality increases as the father's support declines (Exhibit 5).

18. **Environmental Factors:** poor housing is directly linked to the incidence of many childhood illnesses: Poor housing conditions are associated with high rates of admission to hospital and higher morbidity and mortality in adult life (Ref 11). Busy roads also pose risks. On average one child under 15 dies on the road every day and the risk of both injury and death is related to economic disadvantage (Ref. 10).

Exhibit 5
INFANT MORTALITY BY TYPE OF BIRTH REGISTRATION, ENGLAND AND WALES 1990
Infant mortality increases as the father's support declines

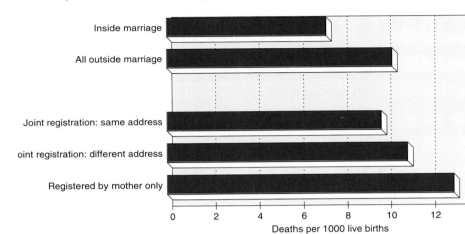

Source: Caroline Woodroffe et al

19. A survey of the health and lifestyle of Londoners (Ref. 12) illustrates the cumulative impact of different threats to well-being. Where none was present, the chances of a child being reported ill were very small - less than one in ten. Where all were present, the probability of being ill was over 95 per cent (Exhibit 6). Additionally, analysis by Bebbington and Miles illustrates how the accumulation of a different set of factors increases the chances of a child being looked after by a local authority some time within the first 17 years of life (Ref. 13) (Exhibit 7, overleaf). There is, however, a striking difference between the two illustrations. Whereas a child in the London survey, subject to all the circumstances listed, is 95% likely to be reported ill, child B in exhibit 7 is still very unlikely to be looked after by the local authority hence posing greater challenges in needs assessment for local authorities.

Exhibit 6
INFLUENCES ON A CHILD'S WELL-BEING
The cumulative impact of different threats to well-being

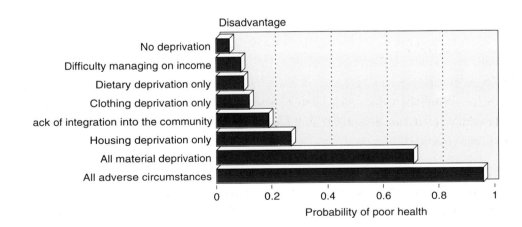

Source: King's Fund Institute, unpublished analysis of data from The Survey of Londoner's Living Standards, 1986.

Exhibit 7
INFLUENCES ON A CHILD'S WELL-BEING
The accumulation of factors increases the chances of being 'in care' (pre Children Act) at some time before age 17

CHILD 'A'	CHILD 'B'
– Aged 5 to 9,	– Ages 5 to 9,
– No dependence on social security benefits,	– Household head receives income support,
– Two parent family,	– Single adult household,
– Three or fewer children,	– Four or more children,
– White,	– Mixed ethnic origin,
– Owner occupied home,	– Privately rented home,
– More rooms than people.	– One or more persons per room.
Odds are 1 in 7,000	**Odds are 1 in 10**

Source: Bebbington and Miles/Department of Health

IMPLICATIONS FOR SERVICE DELIVERY

20. The evidence summarised above indicates that the well-being of children depends on a wide range of factors, many of which are outside the responsibility of health and social services. Nevertheless, both can try to influence those who do have a responsibility for housing, education, transport and leisure facilities. Under the Children Act, social services authorities may request such agencies to assist with the provision of services.

21. Parents also play a key role. Most recognise when their child is ill and needs professional care, or when they themselves need advice, and most will actively seek it. Their needs, and those of their children, are addressed by services available to everyone: primary health care, the provision of information and advice on how to promote the well-being of their children, and by professional health surveillance to check the presence of a small range of threats to the children's well-being. However, some families need rather more help. Greater geographical mobility, smaller families and growth in lone parenthood may all mean young parents are less likely to have the same network of support and opportunities for acquiring parenting skills that the traditional extended family provided.

22. Children can be affected in various ways. They may become physically, emotionally, mentally or socially underdeveloped through a lack of adequate care. As such children grow, their development or behaviour may cause concern unless the underlying problems are addressed. They may become disturbed or delinquent. Poor housing and a poor environment also increase the risk of ill health and accidents (Ref. 10). **Family support** may be required if such children's well-being is to be safeguarded.

23. In exceptional circumstances, children may become seriously neglected or abused, (particularly if their parents were themselves abused or rejected as children), and may be in need of **child protection**. About 25,000 children a year are placed on the child protection register. If families can no longer look after their children or provide them with adequate care they may need to be **looked after** in foster homes or residential care. There are about 55,000 such children.

24. Even more help may be needed for those born with a disabling condition or injured in childhood - some 3% of all children under 16. Such help may range from early detection (which, with resulting services, may reduce the severity of the handicap) to services which provide families with additional help, aids and adaptations. The provision of therapy, or activities to stimulate development provided through nurseries, family centres and in the child's own home, may also alleviate handicaps and the stress on families of caring for a child with disabilities.

25. When a child or young person is placed in an alternative home, the social services authority has a responsibility to ensure that the experience is beneficial and not more damaging than leaving the child with his or her family. Part of that responsibility lies in ensuring that they have proper access to health and other services, particularly education.

26. The responsibilities of local authorities do not cease when young people leave their care and become young adults. Many require preparation for independence and support after they are on their own. Responsibility for 'befriending and advising' those who have left care does not cease until a young adult has reached the age of 21 (which is still much younger than most young people cease to enjoy significant support from their families).

SPENDING AND SERVICE PATTERNS

27. Taken together, community health and social services for safeguarding the well-being of children cost approximately £2 billion per year in England and Wales, of which three quarters is spent by local authorities (Exhibit 8). In the NHS in 1991/92 approximately £295 million was spent on paediatric services in the community (excluding community dental services), of which about 56% was spent on 'development assessment' and 31% on 'other professional advice and support'. In addition a further £85 million was spent on payments to GPs for the provision of

Exhibit 8
COMMUNITY HEALTH AND SOCIAL SERVICES EXPENDITURE ON CHILDREN IN ENGLAND AND WALES
Services cost approximately £2 billion a year

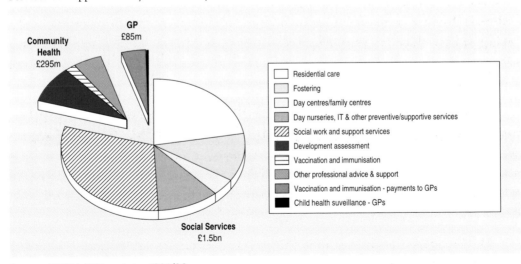

Source: CIPFA PSS statistics 1991/92
DH FR22 Returns 1991/92
FHSA Annual Accounts 1991/92
Welsh office

13

immunisation and child health surveillance. In the past most community units did not identify costs by client group although this is now beginning to change with the need for more precise costings. It is not possible, therefore, to compare expenditure in different health authorities on such activities as child health clinics or the health visitor input to the community child health service.

28. Spending by social services departments on children is currently about £1.5b per annum, which is just over one third of the social services budget. Residential care is much the most expensive form of provision, but as the number of children in such care has been falling, its overall cost now forms less than a quarter of the total spent on children. In 1991/92 the average weekly gross cost (excluding capital charges) of a child in a typical English local authority community home was £659 compared with £128 for a child boarded out with foster carers. These averages should be treated with some caution, however, since expenditure on recruitment and support of foster carers is excluded from the foster care costs (estimated by the Commission to be £25 per child per week). They also mask a range of costs between different types of authorities (Exhibit 9) although it must be remembered that costs of both types of accommodation are likely to rise for children with more problems. In particular, residential care may vary from a preferred option for some young people who are moving toward independence, to a highly expensive resource aimed at accommodating very disturbed and delinquent teenagers. Together, residential care and foster payments account for nearly 70% of the budget for direct services for children (i.e. excluding social work).

Exhibit 9
GROSS WEEKLY COSTS OF RESIDENTIAL AND FOSTER PLACEMENTS 1991/92
A range of costs between different types of authority

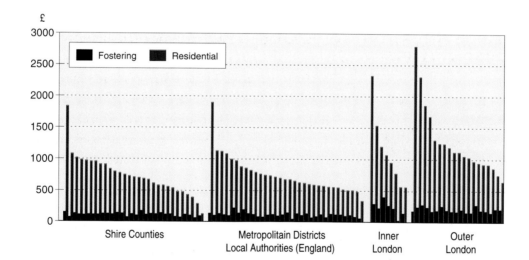

Source: Department of Health Key Indicators of Local Authority Social Services 1991/92 (England)

29. It is more difficult to identify expenditure for supporting families and for preventing a difficult family situation from deteriorating to the point where a child needs to be protected or looked after by the local authority. Day care for under fives accounts for about 16% of the budget but elements of other services may also be used to support a family. Identifying the cost of field

14

social work allocated to children's services is similarly problematic as most authorities, in their accounts, have not split this work between client groups.

30. In both health and social services the pattern of provision has been changing in recent years but in neither are statistics sufficiently precise to describe these changes accurately. In the case of health, with the exception of immunisation, there are no national data on what the resources used actually achieve. Prior to 1992, in the absence of a national programme of health surveillance which involves screening for specific disabilities and checking for developmental delays, authorities or individual professionals went their own way in choosing both the programme of surveillance and its method of execution. A number of studies during the 1980s revealed that much routine surveillance was carried out to a poor standard following programmes that were without justification. In 1992 the Department of Health recommended a programme of surveillance (Ref. 14) based on work by a committee chaired by Professor David Hall, and published as *Health for All Children* (Ref. 15) which suggested a reduction in the number of routine procedures.

31. The method of provision has also changed. Since the introduction of the new GP contract in 1990, increasing numbers of GPs are taking responsibility for immunisations and the basic programme of child health surveillance. Within some family health services authorities (FHSAs) over 90% of GPs are now 'accredited' to carry out this work (most of it undertaken by health visitors working in the GP practice), reducing the need for it to be undertaken at clinics provided by or on behalf of district health authorities. However, the exact number of GPs actually providing surveillance is not readily available. Overall, 40% of children are not yet on the lists of accredited GPs. Children may receive services from a variety of sources including GPs, clinical medical officers (CMOs), health visitors or people with special training in particular areas such as audiology. Working patterns vary from area to area and the number of staff employed in community child health services also varies significantly.

32. These changes in both the content and the method of delivery of child health services reflect both clinical judgement that some of the checks which have traditionally been included in surveillance may not be required, and recognition that a selective approach to surveillance may be adopted once the core programme included in the second edition of the Hall report has been delivered. A number of studies have shown that surveillance identifies only a small number of cases over and above those already known to the child's general practitioner and originally identified by their parents. A recent survey (Ref. 16) concludes that 'parents are far more effective than professionals in the early diagnoses of a wide range of physical and sensory impairments'.

33. For children aged under five many of the core checks are carried out by health visitors. In many areas, health visitors are attached to GP practices and work with the GP population although they remain accountable to the unit or trust employing them. From April 1993, fundholding GPs have been able to purchase community nursing including health visiting from trusts or units. Although some research data exists, there is very little routine information available on the work done, particularly in the area of family support or parenting advice.

34. Most of the other services for children are provided by NHS trusts or directly managed units. Most districts have child development centres (CDCs) from which assessments and support for children with disabilities and their families are co-ordinated: and they also provide a range of other services including audiology, the school health service and support to social services in cases

of abuse. But again, very little information is available on a national basis about what is done and by whom. Small-scale studies however have revealed a variety of patterns.

35. The available statistics on social services do not provide a reliable guide to the overall distribution of resources, nor to the way they are employed. Until now there have been no routine returns showing the proportion of social work which is attributable to work with children nor how it is actually used.

36. However changes in the pattern of provision are apparent. The number of children in the care of local authorities has fallen in recent years from 95,000 in 1980 to 55,000 in 1992. The proportion looked after in residential care has also declined markedly, from 29% in 1981 to 19% in 1992, reflecting the realisation that children's well-being is best served if they can be supported in their own families if at all possible and the belief that fostering is a better option for many children if the local authority has to assume responsibility for their welfare. It is also usually cheaper. The number of children in residential accommodation as a percentage of all children looked after varies significantly, however, between authorities (Exhibit 10) as does the overall rate of children 'looked after'.

Exhibit 10
CHILDREN 'LOOKED AFTER'
The number of children in residential accommodation as a percentage of all children looked after varies significantly.

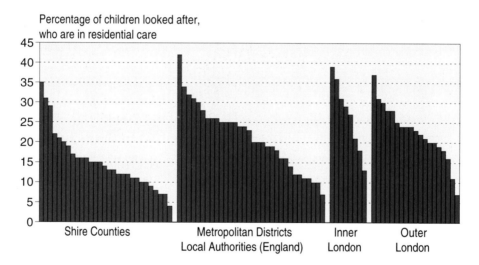

Source: Department of Health key indicators of local authority social services 1991/92 (England)

37. There has been no information nationally, however, about the patterns of service use by children and whether they have changed. For instance, there is no information about how many placement changes a child has while being 'looked after', how long a child remains on the child protection register, how many child protection referrals are made and how many children are re-referred. Certain information on the careers of children is now being collected by Department of Health.

38. This general absence of information is symptomatic of indifferent management and control of services, as described in the next chapter.

Joint

2. The Service Response - Problems Identified

39. This chapter explains the major problems with services currently provided. These are reflected in the light of the three general principles set out in the Introduction: focusing services on needs, providing positive outcomes, and developing partnerships between agencies and with parents. The services are grouped into three sections. Firstly, those activities for which both health and social services have responsibilities; secondly, services provided by health agencies; and thirdly those provided by social services alone (Exhibit 11). Findings are based on studies of eight health and eight social services authorities visited together with evidence from published research and discussions with experts in the field.

Exhibit 11
SERVICE PROVISION
Both health and social services have responsibilities for some activities.

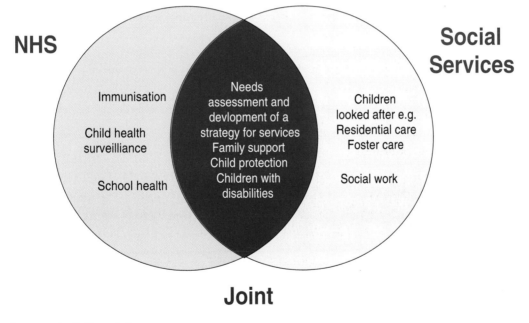

NHS

Social Services

Immunisation

Child health surveilliance

School health

Needs assessment and devlopment of a strategy for services
Family support
Child protection
Children with disabilities

Children looked after e.g. Residential care Foster care

Social work

Joint

Source: Audit Commission

JOINT ACTIVITIES
FORMULATING STRATEGY

40. Parents, health authorities, FHSAs, GPs, social services and education authorities and voluntary bodies share a common concern for the well-being of children. For this concern to be realised effective links must exist between them. This may mean that information is shared or passed on appropriately, or that different authorities develop joint programmes with agencies

Joint

actively working together. The Children Act intends that agencies should work in partnership with each other and with parents. It requires social services to safeguard and promote the health and development of children. Much of the community child health service is devoted to the same concerns.

41. Despite these common concerns and overlapping responsibilities, progress towards an inter-agency strategic approach to the full range of children's services has been disappointing except where it is mandatory. Only two out of eight authorities visited had a common strategic approach to planning for children in need. Various reasons were cited for this: changing agency structures, constant changes to personnel engaged in joint negotiations, a lack of skill and resources, and each agency withdrawing to its core business and wary of joint ventures. Of the two authorities visited that were actively developing a joint approach for children in need, one had a (pilot) joint approach for agreeing definitions, priorities, criteria and extent of need. Department of Health guidance is very firm on a joint approach to child protection - co-ordinated through the area child protection committees (ACPCs) - and considerable progress in this area has been made as a result. A mandatory requirement that services for children under the age of eight must be reviewed by education and social services together has ensured that joint action has been taken in this area. However, only a quarter of social services authorities visited had also involved health authorities, despite the considerable involvement of community child health services with children under eight. There was no indication that parents or the voluntary and private sectors had been involved at a strategic level with decisions on the rest of children's services.

42. If agencies are to develop a joint strategy in which all have responsibilities, a number of actions must be taken. Needs must be defined and prioritised; and risk indicators should be identified and the extent of needs measured. Progress has been patchy, as described below.

Defining needs and priorities

43. The first task is to define the 'needs' that authorities should be addressing and to target services accordingly. Some services are being offered to everyone when a selective approach would be more appropriate; but even targeted services may be provided unnecessarily. They may be imprecisely focused, or miss those who need them because they are focused inaccurately. Authorities must also identify 'risk indicators' in order to guide targeted support accurately to where it is most needed.

44. A survey for the Children Act Report 1992 (Ref. 17) indicated that nearly all 60 responding social services authorities had adopted similar systems for defining children in need. At social services authorities visited by the Audit Commission, all but one had a broad definition of needs and five out of eight had defined priorities. Highest priority was given to children already being looked after or involved in child protection work; but the survey found that only a few authorities had specified known, adverse situations - such as homeless families in bed and breakfast accommodation - as risk indicators of need (Exhibit 12). Below the highest priorities, authorities had generally failed to define need in precise terms.

45. As they stand, however, most statements are not very helpful as a basis for practical measurement of needs and assessment of their distribution within the population. Many are a

Joint

Exhibit 12
RISK INDICATORS OF CHILDREN IN NEED
A minority of authorities had defined a range of known adverse situations as risk indicators of need.

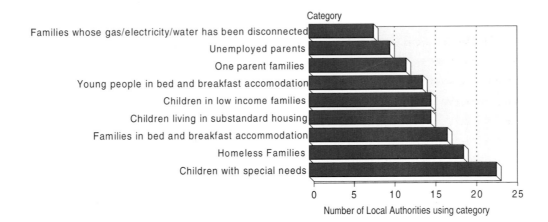

Source: Aldgate/Tunstill/McBeath. No. of authorities = 60

confused mix of priorities, such as a child suffering abuse, and situations where such a risk may exist (families living on benefits, for example).

Measuring the extent of needs

46. Not surprisingly given the absence of clear definitions of need, little work has been done to apply the definitions and to assess the number of children and families with needs. Authorities are apprehensive lest they uncover needs they are unable to meet. In addition, resources are constrained and few staff are available to undertake an assessment. During the course of the study, however, two authorities visited began experimenting with ways of assessing needs.

47. Only one social services authority visited was undertaking work on defining and measuring needs jointly with health (or other agencies) although one other had involved health in identifying local needs as part of the statutory review of services for children aged under eight. Research indicates that health agency staff may not yet have a sufficient understanding of the Children Act definition of children in need (Ref. 17), and health commissioners visited during the study had made little progress on their own in defining or measuring such needs. Resources (and expertise) are scarce.

48. Despite the lack of assessment, social services authorities visited were found to be developing new strategies for children's services; but without a firm grounding in an assessment of needs, such strategies are likely to continue to be service-centred and reactive. Traditionally, social services child care has focused on the crisis intervention of child protection work and on children 'looked after'. This is understandable given stringent budgets and potential tragedies if anything goes wrong. However, the Department of Health has advised social services authorities that it is unacceptable to provide little more than a re-active service engaged in crisis interventions which effectively denies support to other children in need. Social services support is focused too narrowly at present. The new responsibility for 'children in need' is often regarded conceptually by field social workers as a new 'service' with a low priority that does not involve statutory child

Joint

protection - but prevention should be better than cure. An investment in more pro-active services should improve the possibility of reducing the need for crisis intervention.

49. Only two health authorities visited had undertaken a comprehensive needs assessment for community services for children (Exhibit 13). Health visitors provide the main community contact with families whose children are well, providing support to individuals and to groups. Block contracts are still the norm, however, and health visiting requirements continue to be specified in terms of the number of total 'face to face' contacts rather than by the needs of specific groups within the community.

Exhibit 13
PROGRESS IN COMMISSIONING COMMUNITY CHILD HEALTH SERVICES
Only one had identified the needs of children

Authority	1	2	3	4	5	6	7	8
Strategic view	✔	✗	✔	✗	✔	✗	✗	✔
Needs assessment	✔	✗	✔	✗	✗	✗	✗	?
Contract specification	✗	✗	✗	✗	✗	✗	✗	✗
Inform./monitoring	✗	✗	?	✗	✗	?	✗	✗
Links with others	✔	✗	✔	✗	✔	?	?	✗
Quality assurance	?	✗	✗	?	?	✗	?	?

✔   Significant progress made by commissioners

?   Some progress made(but generally made by the provider or not disseminated)

✗   No significant progress made by the commissioners

Source: Source: Audit Commission analysis of authorities visited

50. The result is that resources do not match need in authorities. There is little correlation between the numbers of senior and clinical medical officers (S/CMOs) and the Jarman under privileged area (UPA) score - a proxy for need. Similarly, there is little correlation between the numbers of school nurses or health visitors and relative deprivation as measured by unemployment rates (Exhibit 14). Indeed, work by the York Social Policy Research Unit (Ref. 19) shows that health visitor caseloads have been determined historically.

OPERATIONAL AREAS OF COMMON INTEREST

51. For most children, whose needs for health or social services are straight forward, services can be provided in isolation from each other. For example, in the case of the national programme of immunisation, the main task for the NHS is to ensure as high a take-up as possible among all children. But in several areas there are important links between health and social services for children (as well as other public services - particularly education and the youth justice system):

Exhibit 14
LEVELS OF STAFFING RELATED TO POPULATION NEEDS
There was little correlation between the numbers of health visitors and relative deprivation as measured

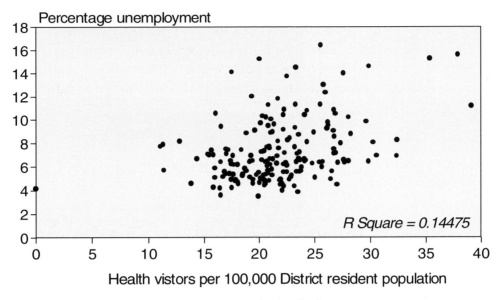

Source: *1991 Census and health service indicators 1990/91 (England)*.

— **Support for the family:** as both agencies now have responsibilities for the health and development of children, there is considerable potential for duplication between health services and social services. Each provides advice, counselling, assistance with parenting skills, and organises support from voluntary bodies, other families and play for children.

— **Child protection:** health and social services both have responsibilities in the prevention and detection of abuse and the subsequent response to its identification;

— **Support for children with a disability:** the most clearly recognised area of common interest is support for the child with disabilities. Health, social services and education are important sources of help.

Family support

52. The need for family support is widely accepted, but not well defined. While there is evidence that some parents need help, there is little research which identifies either the number of families needing help or type of support required. Not only that, there are a number of different professional groups, voluntary bodies and services all providing 'family support' in different ways, including health visitors, family centres, nuseries, social services and parent volunteers. Not surprisingly, therefore, the situation is very confused in practice.

53. For example, the activities of health visitors are not well targeted. Many new mothers, regardless of individual need, receive a variety of routine home visits or requests to attend child health clinics. Indeed, some research (Ref. 20) indicates that parents more likely to be in need can be less likely to receive a home visit or attend a clinic (Exhibit 15, overleaf).

Joint

Exhibit 15
HOME VISITS
Parents more likely to be in need can be less likely to receive support

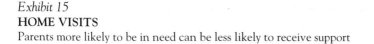

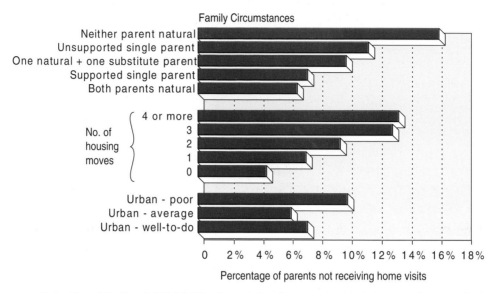

Family Circumstances

- Neither parent natural
- Unsupported single parent
- One natural + one substitute parent
- Supported single parent
- Both parents natural

No. of housing moves
- 4 or more
- 3
- 2
- 1
- 0

- Urban - poor
- Urban - average
- Urban - well-to-do

0 2% 4% 6% 8% 10% 12% 14% 16% 18%

Percentage of parents not receiving home visits

Source: Butler N, and Golding J, 1986 (eds). From birth to five: a study of the behaviour of a national cohort. Pergamon, Oxford.

54. Health visitors at authorities spend about 30% of their time working with families with young children, excluding time spent in health surveillance checks (Exhibit 16), but it is not always clear how or why these families are targeted. Of thirty health visitors interviewed, two thirds had no access to GP practice population profiles which should help them to identify families with needs. Profiles that were available showed only the age and sex of the population, except for six that recorded some information on illness. Only one indicated any further needs. Health visitors were also unable to summarise the needs prevalent in their own caseloads. One agency had introduced criteria specifying levels of activity, but they were subjective and fluctuated according to workload. Health visitors for their part, were un-

Exhibit 16
ACTIVITIES OF HEALTH VISITORS
An average of 30% of their time is spent with families with young children, excluding time spent on health surveillance policy

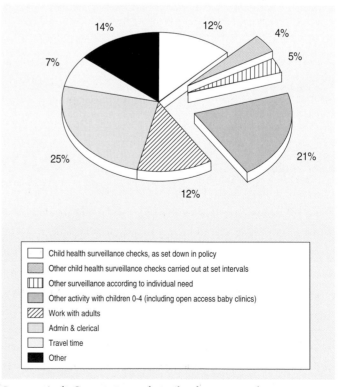

	Child health surveillance checks, as set down in policy
	Other child health surveillance checks carried out at set intervals
	Other surveillance according to individual need
	Other activity with children 0-4 (including open access baby clinics)
	Work with adults
	Admin & clerical
	Travel time
	Other

Source: Audit Commission analysis of authorities visited

22

able to demonstrate how they set priorities. At only one agency visited were there clearly recorded links between an assessed need and the pattern of contact made with a family. The commissioner at another authority had specified that deprived localities were to be targeted, but this had not happened in practice, as health visitors lacked confidence to focus their activity. The lack of monitoring or management information meant commissioners were not aware of these problems. Health visitors' activity or workload were not managed by community health managers at any of the provider agencies visited. But as health visitors look for families with high needs it makes sense to direct them to where such needs are most likely to be found. They should be encouraged to move from historical patterns of universal service delivery to a more focused approach.

55. Some family support and health promotion activities are carried out by health visitors working with groups of parents. Once again there was little demonstrated, assessed or measured need for the work. Out of a total of 69 types of activities undertaken by health visitors across all trust or units visited during the study, only four were explicitly required by the contract with commissioners, nine were set by the community trust or unit and eight were run because health visitors perceived a need in the population. The extent, or level of priority or need for the other 48 activities could not be demonstrated but were undertaken nonetheless for historical reasons or to satisfy a special interest of the health visitor.

56. The lack of clarity about needs, priorities and actions can lead to confusion and duplication between health visitors and social services staff. Health visitors were found to be giving advice on benefits and organising social activities to improve mothers' morale and parenting skills while social services family centres, which have been developing following the Children Act, were found to be undertaking similar tasks and sometimes those traditionally undertaken by health visitors. The teaching of parenting skills to parents attending family centres is seen as an important function; and in some cases parents may need counselling, particularly where they were themselves abused or neglected as children. This work is sometimes conducted by nursery nurses, who are broadening their remit and increasingly working with parents; but without proper training their expertise in this area is questionable. Formal developmental checks are sometimes also conducted by nursery nurses at family centres: at one centre visited they expressed satisfaction when health visitors confirmed their results with similar tests, apparently unaware of the unnecessary duplication of effort. These developments appeared unco-ordinated although there were examples of health visitors being invited to give specific talks to groups of mothers at family centres. Gaps and over-laps could result if there are no joint strategic and operational agreements on objectives, roles and responsibilities.

57. Although there is also some lack of clarity about the respective roles and objectives of nurseries and family centres, social services are generally more successful than health authorities at focusing support on individuals with identified needs. But they face a dilemma where facilities such as nurseries and family centres cater solely for 'targeted' families: receipt of support can become stigmatising making families reluctant to attend. Where they cater for a mix of non-re-ferred and referred families, a lack of space may deny support to families with high needs who might otherwise be referred.

58. Because of the pressure of child protection work, field social workers have little spare time for work with other 'children in need' who require support other than child protection.

Joint

Families with such children may need to seek help through another source if they are to gain access to nursery places for example. Social services nurseries nearly always take children who are regarded to be in need, but these children may not necessarily be at a high risk of abuse or neglect. Nurseries mostly operate their own criteria, and referrals are accepted from health visitors as well as field social workers.

59. Part III, section 17 of the Children Act, which sets out social services responsibilities for children in need, makes provision for a budget to be used in a pro-active way to support families and children. Providing a 'section 17 budget' was the only attempt by all authorities visited to meet their wider responsibilities for children in need in a flexible manner. At present few people at a local level seem to appreciate the difference between this budget and budgets previously provided under section 1 of the Children Act 1980, which allowed payments to be made in a crisis to prevent a child from immediately coming into care. Information on the levels of section 17 expenditure (let alone its scope) was unavailable in some of the authorities visited. There were, in some cases, other resources available for family support, but these were controlled centrally and social workers were unable to assemble services to meet individual needs.

60. Outcomes from family support provided by health authorities are difficult to demon-strate, particularly where there is no assessed need and programmes of support are not evaluated. As a result, activities may not be well targeted and scarce resources can be wasted as a result. There is little to be gained in making repeated routine contacts with healthy families who have adequate parenting skills. With one exception, health visitor records reviewed in the study did not show clearly what was being achieved through contacts with families. Programmes of support provided by some social service family centres and nurseries were found to be more clearly focused and linked to outcomes. Because resources are constrained, and the number of families in need is always greater than the number of places available, programmes are time-limited. The study team visited some where progress is reviewed weekly with parents and positive results are reported. There is little follow-up, however, to see whether improvements are maintained after the programmes have ended.

61. At authorities visited by the study team most family support was provided by profes-sionals. Research by Theresa Smith (Ref. 21), however, suggests that parents who make use of family centres and whose needs are high mostly wanted somewhere for their children to meet and play, and somewhere for themselves to meet other parents for support and social contact. Support from professionals was placed low in importance. Such drop-in facilities, providing a chance for social contact and support, were not necessarily available at all the social services authorities visited. Although 'Homestart' - support for parents by trained community volunteers - was subsidised by two authorities, the only 'non-professional' family support available at all social services authorities visited was sponsored childminding. Voluntary bodies make an important contribution to family support, but there was a five-fold variation in the proportion of social services budgets spent on voluntary agencies to fund family support at authorities visited. Research also suggests that parents value support from other parents in the health and develop-ment of their babies.

62. In conclusion, family support work, like joint collaboration and assessment of needs at a strategic level, is not well co-ordinated. The role of health visitors is ambiguous vis-a-vis some

social services staff. Needs, actions and outcomes are frequently unrecorded and unclear, and stated criteria for levels of intervention with families and children can be vague. While social services work is necessarily more focused, as authorities do not provide universal support, it mostly takes the form of reactive, crisis intervention. Provision of support is still service-driven rather than needs-led and interventions with individual children are not always working towards clear outcomes.

Child protection

63. By its nature, child protection work should be very focused but it can sometimes be difficult to identify why it is being undertaken. Recent research by Jane Gibbons et al (Ref. 22) on child protection referrals, investigations and registrations indicated that up to two thirds of referrals investigated were dropped before being considered for registration at a case conference. There was no suggestion that these referrals were dropped inappropriately, raising questions about the ways in which authorities respond to such referrals. Were criteria and risk indicators - if any - too imprecise to predict that a situation warranted registration rather than some other response? It was difficult to tell at most of the authorities visited as there was no routine collection of information on the number and type of referrals and their progress through investigation.

64. Collaboration on child protection between agencies overseen by multi-agency area child protection committees is strongly advised by the Department of Health in *Working Together* (Ref. 23). As a result, co-ordination between professionals on child protection was more apparent at authorities visited than in other areas of activity, although the involvement of GPs and teachers in child protection proceedings was a problem. Progress has also been made at these authorities in working in partnership with parents. Parents are now invited to child protection case conferences, although in some authorities visited they were not yet routinely allowed to attend the whole of the conference.

Support for children with a disability

65. The third group of services that requires a joint approach involves children with a disability and their families. The needs of these people are often overlooked or marginalised. Children with a disability should be seen as 'children' first and 'disabled' second. Some of their needs will be similar to those who are not disabled but some will be specific to their disability. Such children may require services indefinitely and their parents may need support in their own right.

66. Children with disabilities are a precise (but not homogeneous) group identified as 'in need' specifically by the Children Act – although disability is not defined. Social services authorities are aware that some action should be taken to develop support for them. Health authorities, traditionally more involved with this user group, are more likely than social services to have some estimate of prevalence in their public health reports. There are few indications from either agency, however, that the pattern of service delivery is changing in response to the Act.

67. The Commission has conducted a survey among parents of children with a disability across the age range, and in some cases the children themselves have contributed. 131 families were interviewed. Impairments varied greatly and some children had more than one. The aim

of the survey was to learn parents' views of the support they have received from health and social services (Exhibit 17).

Exhibit 17

COMMISSION SURVEY AMONGST PARENTS OF CHILDREN WITH A DISABILITY.
A selection of parents' views on the support they have received.

Stresses on families

— 'My marriage broke up through it'

— 'My youngest child has had to do things for himself because I have had so little time for him'

Services to help 'could do better...'

— 'The GP told me I was a fussy, over-protective mother'

— 'They would belittle problems I was having with her'

— 'I was told I was neurotic and that there was nothing wrong with her'

— 'If they could accept that mums do notice these things. Mums do know most of the time if their child is not right'

— '... be truthful. We really do need to know what to expect'

However, it wasn't all bad news...

— 'The family doctor... he helped me to cope'

— 'The sister on the ward and the social worker... they would listen to me and had time for me'

— 'When she started school, all the services fitted in at the school, with a helper'

Source: Audit Commission survey

68. Only one social services department visited had a clear strategy for disabled children and none yet had assessments of overall needs. Unless they specialised in children with a disability, child care social workers had little involvement except where accommodation was concerned. (This did not include respite care which was accessed separately.) In addition, although there was both a willingness and, in most centres visited, an ability to accept disabled children in nurseries and family centres, they were not present unless disabilities appeared specifically amongst criteria for admission. Children with disabilities were most noticeably absent in services available to all children (including the child protection register) in those authorities where responsibility for them resided in the adult disability service. They have a legitimate place in all services but are central to none, and their needs, and those of their families, are easily marginalised. Mainstream services do not always recognise them and information on need, and outcome, is difficult to collect, categorise and use.

69. The need for a partnership with parents is thrown into sharp relief when there is a disabled child in the family. In most cases the parents are the main carers. The needs can be long-standing and multiple and their enduring nature may require adjustments, both physical and

social, by carer and child. It is therefore encouraging that parents of children with a disability are often regarded as partners by social services and are involved in individual service planning. The Commission's survey, however, indicated that parents were unhappy with the amount of information and advice provided, particularly when an impairment was first diagnosed. Parents with older children also felt a particular lack of partnership with health and social services when it came to coping with the additional problems attending adolescence. Three quarters of all parents with teenage children in the survey raised this as a significant issue.

70. Parents are frequently the first to detect that their child is not developing normally. In the survey sample, 40% of parents were the first to identify that there was a problem but over half of them were not believed or taken seriously by the professional to whom they turned for advice. GPs were cited most frequently as failing to take parents' concerns seriously. Sixty per cent of GPs have hospital-based paediatric training but this does not include the recognition of disability, leaving a potential skills gap for some GPs who do not have a special interest in this area.

71. Children with a disability require well co-ordinated services, both between agencies and between disciplines within agencies, if their needs are to be addressed satisfactorily and seamlessly. There were examples at authorities visited of good links between individuals at all levels, reflecting traditional networks. Overall, however, there was little evidence of inter-agency co-ordination at a strategic level, which is perhaps not surprising given the complex system of functions and referrals (Exhibit 18, overleaf), and the lack of coterminosity between health and social services authorities.

72. Only one social services authority out of eight visited had an inter-agency agreement with its corresponding health authority at a strategic level. No social services authority visited in 1992/3 had a register as required under the Children Act although at least two corresponding health authorities had good ones. There were intentions to have joint health and social services registers but in most places little real progress had been made towards this goal. Registers from the different agencies can serve different functions, although they still ought to be linked. One social services authority intended to set up an independent register despite the fact that the local

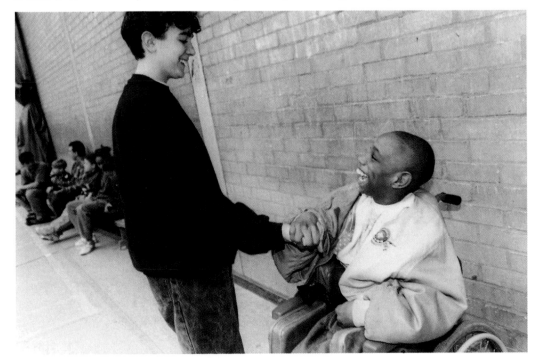

Joint

Exhibit 18
CO-ORDINATING SERVICES FOR CHILDREN WITH A DISABILITY
A complex system of functions and referrals

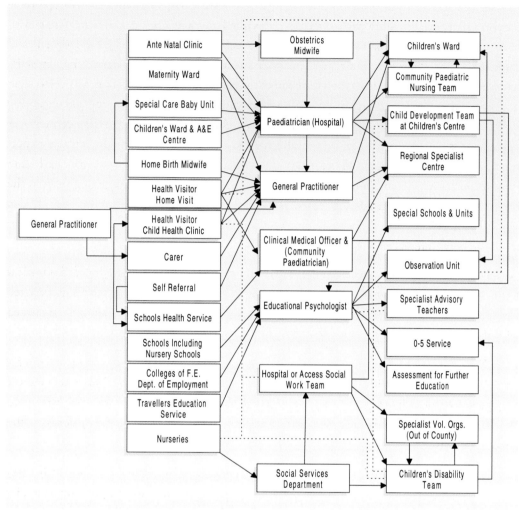

Source : Social Information Systems

health authority had a good one which it was willing to share. Links between social services and education were more common, with half the authorities visited reporting good relationships.

73. The Commission's survey found that only a quarter of parents thought that service delivery was well integrated between agencies. Those parents who were most satisfied had been allocated key workers who acted as the main contact for parents and who facilitated the integration of services.

74. There was considerable friction between agencies – and confusion for parents – about the provision of special aids and equipment. Health, social services and education can all supply similar items but only two authorities visited had tackled the inter-agency issues between health and social services occupational therapy and equipment supplies. Problems included over-bureaucratic approaches, confusion over who could order what equipment, arguments over the source of funding, repeated assessments by different agencies, lack of flexibility in meeting needs, long delays – sometimes so long that the child outgrew the size of item ordered – and no way for parents or children to know whether, or when, they might receive their equipment.

Joint

75. Co-ordination between disciplines within agencies is also important for good delivery of services and difficulties were found within both health and social services authorities visited. In some social services departments it was difficult to identify who was managerially responsible for children with a disability. In health agencies visited, therapy services were often fragmented between the acute and community units and were sometimes provided by generic workers and sometimes by paediatric specialists. District-wide paediatric specialist services can be lost as the service fragments. There were reports of competition between acute and community sectors: in one area both wished to operate child development centres (CDCs) for assessing and organising treatment and support. Families whose disabled young children were attending these centres were liable to miss out on routine contact with health visitors and consequently the routine support normally offered to families. On the other hand, where disability services were arranged other than through a CDC, children's immunisation and screening status might be unknown as the health authority's special needs register tended not to be linked to the child health system. Older, school-age children, tended not to be involved in CDCs and the co-ordination of services was lacking if they were in ordinary schools.

76. Whether children received the frequency or amount of therapy they needed is unclear from the Commission's survey. Physiotherapists, however, were the professionals appreciated most for their help (by 27% of parents in the survey) which suggests that parents were pleased with the nature of this support.

77. There were concerns expressed by professionals about the absence of a clear focus for services where children with disabilities were not attending special schools. There were fears of long delays for such children, given the increased management difficulty of providing services to children who were geographically less easy to reach, and where school staff may not have the depth of understanding of the child's needs.

78. Overall, there is insufficient co-ordination between agencies (and between disciplines) in providing support for children with a disability and their families. The needs of such families can get lost in the confusion and complexity of roles and responsibilities. Where support is being provided through mainstream services available to all children, the special needs caused by the disability can get marginalised. Families with a disabled child may face a lifetime of extra strain, and parents want a greater partnership with professionals in caring for their children.

COMMUNITY CHILD HEALTH: SURVEILLANCE, IMMUNISATION AND SCHOOL HEALTH
SURVEILLANCE AND IMMUNISATION

79. All health authorities carry out checks on children's progress through programmes of 'child health surveillance', but the value of these programmes is questioned (Ref. 24). This is partly because many conditions are identified by parents or GPs on an opportunistic basis, partly because tests are ineffective or badly performed, and partly because early identification is not always valuable. Until further evidence is available, however, the programme recommended in the second edition of *Health For All Children* (Ref. 15) which involves checks at eight weeks, eight months, eighteen months and three years represents professional consensus on procedures, and is recommended by the Department of Health. Most authorities visited were adopting these procedures, but in spite of this, in half the authorities visited, half the health visitors interviewed

were offering extra routine checks for all children without any apparent need or assessment of health gains, and without the commissioner being aware that extra routine work was being done (Exhibit 19).

Exhibit 19
CHILD HEALTH SURVEILLANCE
Extra routine checks for all children

District	8wk	3m	6m	8m	1yr	18m	2yr	3yr	Pre-school
1	○			○		○		○	
2	○	□	□	○	□	○	□	○	□
3				○		○		○	
4				○		○		○	
5	□	□	□	○	□	○	□	○	□
6	□	□	□	○	□	○	□	○	□
7		□	□	○	□	○	□	○	○
8	○	□	□	○	□	○		○	○

○ = *Perceived programme policy*
□ = *Additional programme offered by some HVs as routine*

80. Whatever programmes are being carried out, it is essential that authorities ensure maximum participation, requiring those involved to have an accurate record of coverage, referrals and subsequent action. Following the introduction of the new GP contract in 1990 more GPs give immunisations to pre-school age children. As payments to them are linked to overall uptake, this information is collected by FHSAs. Information is usually also available at community trusts or units. It is not always validated against FHSA records, however, and information is not always accurate. As a result, some parents may not receive timely reminders of immunisations due. Alternatively, staff (often health visitors) may waste time chasing parents whose child appears to have missed an immunisation only to find it has already been given.

81. Information on immunisations and boosters given to school age children is not always available. Only two of the eight authorities visited could supply comprehensive data on coverage. Modules on school health are available as part of the child health information system but many authorities do not have them. Even where they do exist, accuracy is suspect as immunisations are given in a variety of places including schools, GP practices and hospitals. High rates of uptake depend on good quality information.

82. Data were not always available on coverage of the child health surveillance programme. Although computerised child health information systems are widely used, only half the authorities visited were able to supply information on all the pre-school checks. Other authorities had information on only some of the checks, and at several, collection of such information had only recently begun. Information on the results of surveillance (in terms of onward referrals) was available at only two authorities visited. The accuracy of surveillance procedures cannot be monitored if information is not available on the number and appropriateness of referrals.

83. As a probe into the efficiency and effectiveness with which surveillance is conducted, the Commission reviewed the screen for hearing loss. The response varied. Not all authorities could identify coverage and among those that could, the range varied from 52% to 92% of

children. Only one agency could tell as a matter of course how many referrals were true or false positives for sensorineural hearing loss, an irreversible and usually congenital condition. Similarly at only one could they routinely report the ages at referral. Two authorities were able to show, by looking at individual records, the ages at which the condition was detected. At one agency, in the previous year, only a single child out of 10 was identified at the appropriate age. Another agency held an audit of its audiology service and established that in the last five years no case of sensorineural deafness recorded had been picked up by the universal 'distraction test' screen. Inefficient tests are an ineffective screen which not only wastes resources but give children and their parents either a false sense of security or undue cause for alarm. Lack of clear responsibilities for audit in these areas can mean that these issues together with common complaints about the environment in which tests are conducted and training of staff may not be adequately investigated.

84. Immunisation, together with child health surveillance, is increasingly performed by GPs and practice based staff in their own clinics and surgeries. Although the number of GPs accredited for surveillance has increased rapidly over the last three years there was little evidence at agencies visited of collaboration between health authorities, community trusts, units and GPs. Only one authority visited was able to identify how many parents were choosing to attend GP rather than health authority clinics for immunisation. None was monitoring the number of children attending specific clinic sessions. While authorities should have regard for parental choice, under-used clinics waste resources, and should be reduced. Part of the problem is due to uncertainty about the role of the clinics. Some are primarily for immunisation and formal surveillance checks, with parents and children attending by appointment. Others appear less well defined, providing an uncertain mix of family support and surveillance.

GP fundholders

85. The increasing involvement of GPs, both as providers and, where they are fundholders, as commissioners of community child health services has wider implications. Their priorities may be somewhat different from those of commissioning authorities, creating tensions.

86. For example, they sometimes prefer a combined preventive/curative model of health care (which parallels their own) giving rise to combined practice nurse/health visitor posts. This in turn is causing concern to some people who fear that treatment services may crowd out prevention and health promotion activities, undermining the specialist child care focus of health visitors and presenting community units and trusts with conflicting demands. And while GPs bring a better knowledge of local circumstances, concerns are also being expressed that the wider perspective of the commissioning authority with its 'public health' dimension may be put at risk.

87. Part of the reason for giving a bigger role to GPs and for setting up fund holding was to create these very tensions - stimulating debate and discussion about the best way forward. But care is needed to ensure that change is managed constructively.

SCHOOL HEALTH

88. Universal medicals at school entry are beginning to decline in favour of selective examinations. In most authorities visited, systems were haphazard for passing key information from the pre-school surveillance programme to school nurses and medical officers although this may improve when children with parent-held records reach school age. The study team con-

NHS   SSD

ducted a survey of head teachers' views on the school health service in authorities visited. The majority of these that responded regarded the school medical officer (CMO) role as being concerned primarily with conducting medicals, and secondly with liaising with other parts of the NHS and supporting pupils with special needs. In their experience, head teachers did not particularly value school medical officers as providers of advice and health education to students. These functions, together with the giving of advice to staff, were seen as the province of school nurses. School nurses interviewed at authorities, however, found that suitable training for this work was not always available.

89. In conclusion, although services are being reduced to those whose benefit is acknowledged by a consensus of professional opinion, some extra work is still being done which may be of dubious value. Data collection and management systems are not in place to identify low value or poorly performed activities. The role of child health clinics is confused, and there may be some duplication of activities with GP clinics. Collaboration with GPs who are increasingly responsible for immunisation and surveillance is inadequate.

SOCIAL SERVICES: SOCIAL WORK AND CHILDREN LOOKED AFTER
SOCIAL WORK

90. Until recently many authorities used a 'generic model' of social work with social workers working with all client groups. In theory, social workers carried a mixed caseload of children, elderly people or disabled adults. In practice, child protection work tended to dominate. Generic working of this nature is now declining, as implementation of the *NHS and Community Care Act* and *Children Act* has demanded greater specialist knowledge, (although one authority visited still formally operates in this way). But even authorities deploying specialist child care social workers are finding that they are concentrating on a narrow range of services in a reactive way, with little time for other needs (Exhibit 20). As a result, attention given to families or children with less crisis-driven requirements was limited and children with disabilities in particular have missed out. Adolescents leaving care who talked to the study team were critical of the amount and quality of social work they had received as teenagers whilst in care. Resources need to be released or re-organised in order to address these concerns.

91. Strategic decisions on the balance of services, who they will serve and how they will

Exhibit 20
THE ROLE OF CHILD CARE SOCIAL WORKERS
Social workers are concentrating on a narrow range of services in a reactive way

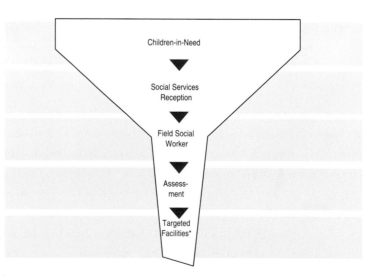

Children-in-Need

Social Services
Reception

Field Social
Worker

Assess-
ment

Targeted
Facilities*

Note: * eg. Social work, Children's homes, Foster parents, Family centres

operate, cannot sensibly be taken without taking into account the role of social workers. They are a significant resource, yet authorities are frequently unaware of the balance of their work on a day-by-day basis. Caseloads are not a good measure of workloads as definitions of what constitutes 'a case' vary and the amount of activity required on any one 'case' can vary significantly. Only two authorities visited were developing weighted workload management schemes to allow senior managers to monitor the balance and type of work between social workers and between teams. One of these authorities found that the workload varied widely (Exhibit 21). This suggests that staff may not be well matched to needs. Those authorities without such a system do not know how well their resources are deployed.

Exhibit 21
FIELD SOCIAL WORKERS' WORKLOAD
Varied widely between different social work teams

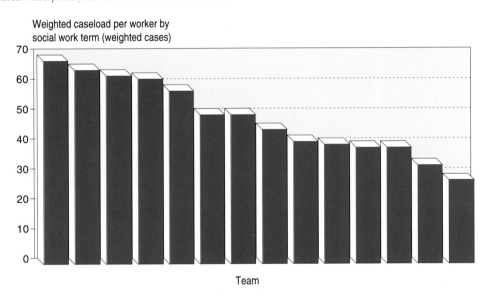

Weighted caseload per worker by
social work term (weighted cases)

Team

Source: Audit Commission analysis of data from a sample authority visited.

CHILDREN 'LOOKED AFTER'

92. Research indicates that both short and long-term outcomes for children looked after by social services can be poor (Ref. 13) particularly when placements in foster or residential care break down. There are a number of risk indicators predicting an increased chance of breakdown identified by research; but such indicators were rarely used at authorities visited.

93. Good assessments and care plans are the key to effective results but guidance was found to be vague. Individual social workers were often left to their own discretion. The Department of Health has supported the production of a format, linked to outcomes, for assessing and reviewing children looked after (Ref. 25), but some authorities commented that it is too detailed and time consuming. Some social workers at authorities visited were unaware of research on outcomes published by the Department of Health (Ref. 13). Others were aware of its existence but were not always able to use its findings. For example, while they were aware that a high number of placement changes for a child is detrimental, in practice they often found it difficult to avoid moves. Information systems are poor and do not allow social workers or managers to monitor outcomes, or risk indicators such as multiple moves, or changes of school.

SSD

94. The education of children looked after is of increasing concern to social services authorities. A rising number of children are being excluded, formally or otherwise, from school, particularly following the introduction of locally managed schools and grant maintained status. The study team undertook a one day census of children in residential care at the authorities visited to identify the proportion not at school for reasons other than for sickness and found it to be between a sixth and a third (Exhibit 22).

Exhibit 22
CHILDREN LOOKED AFTER
The proportion not at school on one day, other than for sickness.

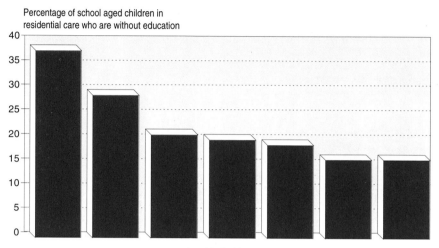

Source: Audit Commission analysis of data - authorities visited

95. There was little evidence that this problem was being addressed rigorously by social services and education departments. Social services departments complained that education departments were not providing alternative education beyond a maximum of five hours home tuition a week, while education staff commented that social services staff failed to involve themselves soon enough with the schools and were not acting as 'concerned parents' addressing issues with the school at a sufficiently early stage. Meanwhile the children missed their education. Some were in the last year of compulsory schooling; others had several years of education ahead of them.

96. In order to prevent children being looked after away from home unnecessarily, social services authorities set up gate keeping panels to approve admissions, particularly to residential care. Considerable friction was evident at authorities visited between social workers and gatekeeping panels. Social workers complained that panels questioned their competence at assessment and care planning; panel members commented that assessments and planning were vague and that some children referred to them were better off at home. Care providers felt that their expertise was under-used when care plans were being prepared. Where the system for making emergency placements allowed social workers to by-pass the panels, there was a danger that it could be over-used in order to avoid the rigours of the panel members' queries.

97. Foster care schemes varied in quality at authorities visited. While some were well thought out and managed, others were less so. Quality varied both in professional management of the service and in information available to social workers. Where fostering officers were

members of area social work teams, social workers found it difficult to locate suitable foster carers if none was available in their local patch. Suitable places for children from about the age of 10 are particularly hard to locate - especially for boys. In one authority visited, some fostering and adoption officers also carried child care caseloads. They found it particularly hard to act effectively in their specialist role. Good foster carers were harder to recruit and retain in schemes where fostering officers were expected to both recruit carers and support more than about 20 (counting couples as one).

98. Every authority visited reported difficulty in providing choice. The existence of vacancies did not mean that there were places suitable for a particular child. Authorities were still grappling with the question of the role of residential care. Social workers were aware that the mix of young people placed in a particular home could have adverse outcomes for those involved but were not always able to make other arrangements. Homes lacked clear objectives and although observation and assessment units no longer formally exist, emergency placements were sometimes in effect, recreating a version of them in practice.

99. Staffing levels were low in a number of residential homes at authorities visited. At one authority four full-time-equivalent staff were expected to provide cover, seven days a week, in homes with six children. The *Pindown experience and the protection of children* (Ref. 26) stressed that one staff member, however experienced, should not be on duty alone with children.

100. Statistics and research have indicated that outcomes for young people leaving care have been poor. Aged 16 or 17 these adolescents have found themselves having to cope on their own several years earlier than most of their more fortunate peers who live with their families. Debt, homelessness, crime and pregnancy have too frequently been their fate. *The Children Act* has laid a responsibility on social services authorities to 'befriend' and 'advise' such youngsters in expectation that the negative effects of youthful independence can be prevented. Schemes to address the needs of this group are mostly new. But two thirds of authorities visited had no procedure to ensure that a leaving care plan was prepared at age 14 or 15 for those children expected to remain the responsibility of the local authority. Children's field social workers remained accountable for young people leaving care at six out of the eight sites. Young people leaving care who talked to the study team were critical that social workers were unable to cope with their needs (and they were refreshingly objective about the problems they presented to their social workers). They also felt social workers did not have time to listen.

SUMMARY OF PROBLEMS

101. To summarise, according to the key principles re-iterated at the beginning of chapter two.

102. **Focusing on needs:** Neither health nor social services authorities have yet determined the extent of relative needs in their areas although some work has been done at a strategic level on definitions and priorities. Until this is done, resources cannot be allocated effectively. As resources are constrained it is important that they should be focused appropriately on needs.

103. **Outcomes:** Objectives of services are frequently vague and outcomes unclear. This is particularly so in community child health services, but also for children looked after by social services.

Joint

104. **Partnership between agencies and with parents:** Despite a number of common concerns and overlapping responsibilities there has been a disappointing lack of collaboration between health and social services authorities on developing an inter-agency approach to the strategic planning for children. At present, there is little common understanding (or procedures) between health and social services authorities on how to interpret the criteria in the Children Act to suit local circumstances. At practitioner level, support offered to families is rarely co-ordinated and there is insufficient understanding by health authority staff of the Children Act definition of children in need. Where co-operation is mandatory or strongly recommended, however, as in child protection, greater progress has been made.

105. Overall the principle of partnership with parents has been accepted by all authorities visited but the degree to which it was being implemented varied. While most authorities did not have a specific policy designed to increase the contribution of parents, community trusts and units were introducing parent-held records and social services were involving parents in case conferences. A start was being made in putting this new principle into practice.

106. The next chapter suggests how the problems identified in chapter two might be addressed. Many authorities recognise the challenges they face and are taking steps to overcome them. Examples of good practice seen by the study team are illustrated in the following pages.

3. Moving Forward

107. The previous two chapters have described some of the needs confronting children and their families, and some of the problems that authorities recognise must be resolved if they are to address those needs. The remainder of this report summarises possible ways forward, first for authorities working together and then for authorities individually.

Exhibit 23

PRODUCING A CHILDREN'S SERVICE PLAN

Authorities should work together to develop a joint children's strategy

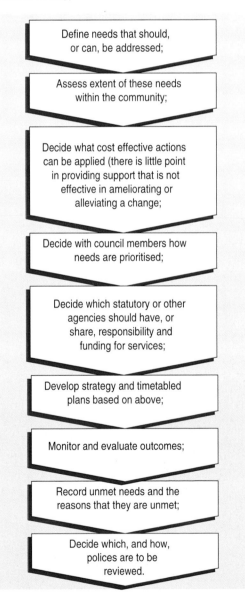

Define needs that should, or can, be addressed;

Assess extent of these needs within the community;

Decide what cost effective actions can be applied (there is little point in providing support that is not effective in ameliorating or alleviating a change;

Decide with council members how needs are prioritised;

Decide which statutory or other agencies should have, or share, responsibility and funding for services;

Develop strategy and timetabled plans based on above;

Monitor and evaluate outcomes;

Record unmet needs and the reasons that they are unmet;

Decide which, and how, polices are to be reviewed.

DEVELOPING JOINT PARTNERSHIPS

108. Both health and social services authorities must adopt a needs-led rather than a service-driven approach. Their common concern for the well-being of children, their overlapping responsibilities, and their common involvement with many children all mean that co-ordinated actions (including co-ordinated commissioning between health, local and family health services authorities) should be the aim.

JOINT ASSESSMENT OF NEEDS AND DEVELOPMENT OF A STRATEGY

109. Health and local authorities should start by jointly defining what they mean by 'need'. Absolute need would be impossible to address – even if such a concept could be described adequately. Therefore, agencies must decide together which needs can, and should, be met by the provision of a range of services.

110. If needs are to be addressed in the most cost-effective way, voluntary bodies as well as other local authority departments such as education, housing, highways and leisure should be involved in developing a children's strategy (Exhibit 23). A method should also be found to incorporate the views of service users. This strategy should be set down in a **children's service**

Joint

plan which should be jointly published by health, social service and education in much the same way as community care plans are now.

111. Assessing the extent of need is new to most authorities. Use should be made of research, mortality and morbidity data to identify areas of deprivation, high unemployment and high numbers of young, unsupported parents (such as in married quarters at military establishments as well as in the civilian community). Often there will be strong associations between all three. Demographic information from the census can be produced for individual electoral wards and can be particularly valuable in helping to assess the prevalence of risk indicators in the population; and directors of public health may have access to other sources of information such as registers of children with a disability. Individual practitioners may have valuable information on need at local level, for example in their practice profiles.

112. Findings from pilot projects assessing the number of children in need in a local community have indicated that:

— the 1991 OPCS census data are accurate at ward level when suitably weighted (Ref. 27). Both professional staff and public consultation can be used to identify specific service needs;

— the work must be carried out in a multi-agency forum with all agencies willing to fund services jointly. Within this framework set by senior management, local forums of middle managers from the major agencies and voluntary bodies can assess local needs effectively.

113. A multi-agency approach, with full support from authority members and a sharing of costs, is proving to be essential. The Welsh Planning Forum has recently issued draft guidance to health authorities on planning for children's services (Ref. 28). It lists the five areas requiring joint action as defining need, assessing its extent, prioritising between needs, identifying the children concerned, and planning appropriate services. Here again, experience so far suggests that total commitment from the top to a joint approach is crucial for success. Within local authorities a corporate approach should involve elected members and the chief executive.

114. Parents are also partners and information gathered directly from them and other user groups should not be overlooked. In one authority visited local groups of parents are involved in the regular planning process for services for children under eight.

OPERATIONAL AREAS OF COMMON INTEREST

115. Health and local authorities must also work together at the operational level to co-ordinate family support, specialist services for children with disabilities, and child protection services (considered in turn below). These services overlap, since family support is provided both to children with disabilities and as part of child protection.

Family support

116. Family support has yet to be widely recognised as a topic requiring joint planning and co-ordination, although there is a high level of agreement that health visitors provide valuable support to families. They have been described as the 'eyes and ears' of social services, able to identify and address needs proactively in a manner not available to social services staff. Unfortunately, it is difficult to demonstrate the value of different health visitor activities or to determine the amount of health visiting required. The only indicator of effectiveness appears to be the many referrals from health visitors to social services for support (including child protection) - and even such a straightforward indicator is rarely quantified, and must instead be gauged from the perceptions of social services staff.

117. Many parents are able to care quite adequately for their children. They should be helped in their task by the provision of good, written information on key aspects of child care backed by a contact point from which further guidance can be obtained. One authority visited operates an out-of-hours help-line at night time and at weekends when the health visitor office is closed. Staffed by health visitors the line is situated in the accident and emergency department of the local hospital. Its budget in 1993 was £25,000 and it may have benefited GPs indirectly by taking calls that would otherwise have gone to them.

118. Regular routine contacts not resulting from an assessment of need should be discouraged. After a universal first visit from a health visitor to each family with a new baby, all further routine visiting, apart from the agreed surveillance programme, should be based on assessed needs against agreed priorities in order to release resources for situations where there are clear needs.

119. Although the absence of tangible evidence that health visitors are effective is a cause for concern, all authorities visited during the study expressed anxiety that any arbitrary and unilateral reductions to health visiting could have serious repercussions for both children and families and to social services. Any reduction could be damaging if introduced without proper assessment or evaluation first. Such evaluation should be undertaken as a matter of some urgency.

120. As well as sharing a common interest in family support, health and social services also share some common activities. Family centres could provide a suitable focus. Many are currently operated by social services departments or voluntary agencies and more are planned. They could to advantage become joint ventures between health, social services, education and voluntary organisations, providing a base for group work with families and children, child health clinics (other than those provided by GPs in their practices), peer support groups (in which mothers support each other), nursery classes and playgroups, counselling and advice on housing and social security benefits and a base for staff making home visits. Placed in appropriate locations they could provide a 'one stop shop' for local communities.

121. It may also be possible to include some child development centre (CDC) activities, such as outpatient consultations or certain treatments, provided appropriate equipment is available. Some new centres have special rooms designed and equipped to provide sensory stimulation for example. Such arrangements would benefit families who live a long way from existing CDCs, and make facilities, which are available to children in general, accessible to children with disabilities.

Joint

122. Multi-purpose centres would bring together the various skills of different professionals, to the potential benefit of families. There may be complications if professionals do not relate to the same populations. An alignment of working patterns between health visitors and social services staff should be relatively straightforward where they serve common areas; but many health visitors are attached to GPs' surgeries (although not necessarily based there) and work only with the people on the GPs' lists. This makes sense for routine immunisation and surveillance of children, particularly where child health clinics are run by GPs at their surgeries. But group support and other 'public health' activities provided by health visitors could be organised to advantage in conjunction with social services on a geographical basis – particularly in inner cities and other areas with high needs. Areas with a significant ethnic population could also benefit from a concentration of skills, since knowledge of the language and the nuances of culture are of great importance and are in short supply. Combining skills and resources allows particular specialist skills such as one-to-one counselling or group work to be developed and used to the full, so helping to ensure that needs are met more cost-effectively.

123. The distinction between family centres and nurseries should be clearly set out. Each unit should know where it fits in with other services and what it aims to achieve with children and families. Structures and training should be appropriate. Intensive intervention work such as specialist training in parenting skills, and counselling should be evaluated for effectiveness. A mix of open access with a quota of referred families is preferable to a closed system but if the latter is operated, drop-in facilities in localities in which there are high needs appear to be welcomed by parents.

124. Few examples have been found of family support co-ordinated through family centres although some have made good progress. One such is Pen Green at Corby in an area with significant needs (Case Study 1). In Oxfordshire, a scheme is under way which provides support and training to parents and children to help them overcome problems with children's behaviour and family relationships (Case Study 2). The provider is a voluntary body, the professional staff have health and psychology qualifications and the venues are family centres. Early results are encouraging.

125. Both research and opinion suggest that lack of confidence, low self esteem and depression are significant causes of poor parenting in areas of high need. There are a number of possible support programmes that authorities can explore. Newpin is a voluntary group with branches in several locations usually financed by either health or social services (and its own trust fund). Parents under stress are supported by others who have previously experienced similar difficulties. It develops self esteem and confidence in parents without creating dependency on professionals. Evaluation suggests that it is successful in reducing the incidence of child abuse and increasing the ability of parents to care for their children without the need for intervention from social services. The cost of a place for a year is about £1000, which compares very favourably with the cost of a foster place at £7000 or a residential place at £30,000 - either of which could be needed if parental stress is not relieved. Homestart is another useful national voluntary group which provides trained, local volunteers who give support and advice to parents.

126. These are examples of national projects. There are other local projects too with good reputations, such as 45 Cope St. (Nottingham). This scheme aims, through group work with

Joint

Case Study 1

PEN GREEN CENTRE FOR UNDER 5S AND THEIR FAMILIES, CORBY

CLOSE CO-OPERATION WITH HEALTH AGENCIES AND OTHERS TO OFFER A
VARIETY OF SUPPORT

Aims – Its aim is to offer a supportive environment, which will help children grow and develop. In some cases this will mean providing the child with stimulation through pre-school education or after school provision; in others it will mean providing parents with additional support in helping their children to develop.

Funding – joint, by Northamptonshire's education and social services departments. Estimates for 1994 suggest a total LA contribution of £280,000. It also has close working relationships with the local health authority. Staffing is multi-disciplinary, with social workers, teachers, nursery nurses and health visitors involved with activities in the centre. In addition, there is a central role for parents themselves, in running some sessions. Much of the work crosses traditional professional boundaries.

Scale – scale of activity is difficult to estimate precisely given the range of activities. However a 'snapshot' suggests:

— Up to 300 adults may pass through the centre each day;

— 59 families use the nursery provision;

— 38 parents use drop-in facilities;

— 38 parents are involved in group work;

— 70 parents use the centre for other purposes.

Activities – various activities are on offer at the centre, both for families who have been referred by health or social services, and for families who simply wish to make use of the facilities on offer at the centre. Children with disabilities are integrated with children who are not disabled.

A nursery – Pen Green offers a nursery where the curriculum has been developed jointly between social services and education. Half of the places are reserved for children or families who are felt to be in need. The remaining places are open, and are allocated on a first-come-first-served basis to children on a waiting list. However, the centre is sited in an area of high needs. There are 39 full time equivalent places, including a small number of places earmarked for children on the child protection register.

Play groups – run by parents but facilitated by staff (25 places).

Support groups – Staff offer some 25 support groups some of which will assist with parents suffering from stress or difficulty that resulted in a referral from the statutory agencies, and others that have been developed in response to the community's own expressed needs. In addition, parents run their own mutual support groups without the participation of staff, using the facilities of the centre, and the staff for advice and support if necessary. There is a crèche facility for parents using groups.

Drop in sessions – There are also baby clinics, adult health advice sessions and other drop in sessions which are developed in response to local needs. Approximately 25 parents and children regularly use the drop in facility at any one time.

Outreach work - staff undertake outreach work with families in their own homes on basis of individual need.

Other activities - specific projects are funded separately and are developed in response to specific needs. These vary year on year and are not part of the 'core' activities of the centre.

41

Joint

Case Study 2
SUPPORT TO PARENTS

OXFORD FAMILY NURTURING NETWORK

Aims – To improve parenting skills and nurturing in families at risk of abusing and neglecting children. Aims to benefit both families with severe difficulties as well as those whose needs are less critical.

Method – The project uses a formal process: 'The Nurturing Program of Parents and Children 4-12' developed in the USA combining parent education and nurturing with support from other parents.

A maximum of ten families are taken through 15 weeks of two-and-a-half hour sessions.

Children and parents, in separate groups, work on similar topics each week.

For example:

— child behaviour management that avoids violence

— importance of praise

— recognising feelings and personal needs

— assertiveness and learning to say 'no'

— handling stress and anger

— development stages of children

— responsibility for own behaviour

— drug and alcohol abuse

— how to increase self esteem.

Adults' group uses handbooks, video, discussion and role play.

Children's group uses discussion, artwork, games, play-acting, puppets and music.

Staffing

The project is run by three part-time co-ordinators: a clinical psychologist, health visitor and clinical nurse specialist.

The co-ordinators train volunteers from the caring professions including teachers, social workers, health visitors and psychologists.

Recruited and trained - 66 volunteers.

Co-ordinators run the parents' group. Volunteers run the children's groups.

Set-up arrangements – The network has charitable status and is independent from health and social services, but collaborates with both.

Support procured from local health and social services authorities and approval secured from Area Child Protection Committee (ACPC).

Funding – Joseph Rowntree Trust

Funds also raised from social services, local charities, business and private donors.

Activity – Each 15 week program is run from different social services family centres and other community centres.

Referrals canvassed from social services, health visitors, primary schools, educational and paediatric psychology services and child psychiatric service.

In 12 months 50 families have attended programmes. Most were one-parent families. Half of the fathers invited to participate have completed the course.

Evaluation so far – Evaluation measures developed and piloted.

American materials and approach are acceptable to participants, with parents reporting high levels of satisfaction.

For those families who persevere with programme there are positive changes. Some families need more support before changes are sustained.

Improvements in children's behaviour, and progress at school reported by some parents.

Social services appreciative of positive changes in some client families.

Evaluation of effect on families to be undertaken.

Budget (1 year) – £85,000 to cover 3 co-ordinators, working three and a half days each per week, plus secretary, plus programme materials.

Future aims – Lack of specific training noted among professionals (e.g. in primary care, schools and social services) on how to manage difficult behaviour shown by children. Aim to develop training in the project's methods nationally.

health visitors, to improve the health of mothers. The work is evaluated by health visitors and the women as it progresses. In addition to specifying projects of this nature – and agreeing to innovative, well designed local initiatives with evaluation built in – authorities can encourage the development of a range of specific programmes for families with specific identified needs. One good practice community trust visited had obtained academic support for its community nurse development unit so that improved and innovative health visitor techniques could be developed. Authorities should be prepared to allow funding for the design and evaluation of experimental programmes which should have clearly specified objectives and methods for evaluation. Those that prove ineffective can then be dropped. In this way a range of effective programmes can be developed over a number of years.

127. The amount and type of family support required will depend on the findings of needs reviews. Authorities will need to think carefully about priorities, and then work out who is going to undertake the resulting programme of action. Almost inevitably, there will need to be some adjustment to resource levels and skill mixes as both the way needs are met and skills are deployed are reviewed across agencies in the light of jointly agreed needs and priorities. In social services authorities in particular, there will need to be some rebalancing. Traditionally, most child care cases have been channelled to social workers, who have acted as 'gatekeepers' for more specialised services.

Joint

128. Following the Children Act, social services have wider responsibilities - requiring a broader approach which may at times not necessarily involve social workers at all. This broader approach allows the diversion of some families to other resources, providing a more proactive service that makes use of a wider range of options (Exhibit 24). It is important that any diversion scheme should be systematically evaluated.

Exhibit 24
A BROADER APPROACH
allows the diversion of some families to other resources

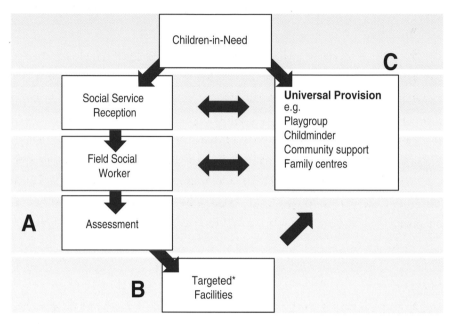

*e.g. Social work, Children's homes, Foster parents, Family centres

129. Such an approach requires a redirection of resources from the traditional areas of activity A and B in exhibit 24 to area C. In theory, effective investment in C should reduce the need for A and B anyway, reducing family stress and the need for crisis intervention; but in practice, such an effect has not yet been properly evaluated. At present most authorities have identified only a 'section 17' budget as highlighted in chapter two (the Children Act gives authorities the power to set up a budget to provide services to children in need, under sec. 17). Section 17 budgets should not necessarily be confined to field social workers. Under-eights' officers, family (resource) centre managers, respite care organisers and others might also be appropriate holders. One authority allocated small, discrete budgets (not termed 'section 17') to such staff for them to provide innovative, individual support. Budgets were all small but staff using them spoke highly of their effectiveness. Strategic direction and operational guidance on the use of section 17 budgets should be improved and linked to the overall distribution of needs within the authority. Field social workers may need educating in handling these budgets as part of the cultural change in children's services. Use of the budgets should also be monitored, both in financial terms and in effectiveness in providing family support.

130. A model of diversion also requires an effective duty system which does not waste social workers' time which could be otherwise engaged to better effect on case work. Some social services authorities, including Cheshire County Council, are experimenting with permanent 'customer reception' teams which include social workers but also have skilled administrative staff, who are able to offer a higher level of advice and guidance to callers than is traditionally expected of receptionists. If referrals cannot be resolved easily, they are given a priority rating and passed to the relevant specialist team. It is important that a mixed team of administrative and social work staff is well trained and supported if they are to provide good quality reception. Procedures must be clear and well understood.

131. Success in diversion will depend on the development of an effective range of alternative services. Such a range should be developed in close co-operation with health and others as discussed earlier, with closer working arrangements, shared facilities, clearer working practices and joint funding of voluntary support – such as Newpin, Homestart, community volunteers - where appropriate. The idea of a 'primary resource' or 'one-stop-shop' family centre could act as a single point of entry to a range of multi-agency support services such as drop-in facilities, peer support groups, nursery, benefits and housing advice, child health and well women clinics, playgroups and after school schemes. Such a model would help to de-stigmatise social services support – a current problem – but would not exclude access to a social worker should it be requested or required.

Child protection

132. Child protection is another topic requiring close inter-agency working and co-operation, as every investigation into the death of a child undertaken since the war has commented on poor liaison between professionals. Area child protection committees (ACPCs) are demonstrating what can be achieved when joint working is given a sufficiently high profile, although greater efforts are needed to secure the co-operation of schools and GPs perhaps through individual approaches to governors, head teachers and GPs.

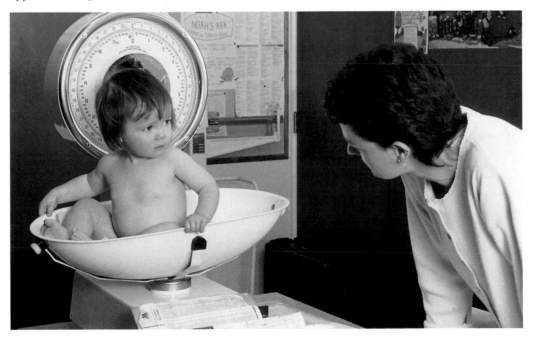

Joint

133. Although roles, responsibilities and procedures at authorities visited had all been reviewed and clarified following the Children Act, there was still a need to improve management information. The number of child protection referrals received by teams, their progress (how many are investigated, how many are dropped and why), the proportion that go to case conference and the proportion registered, should be recorded and the analysis used to inform management, both for decisions on the distribution of resources and as an aid to quality assurance. Software packages which provide most of this information are available.

Support for children with a disability

134. Chapter two has described how services for disabled children are fragmented between different agencies, and their needs marginalised as a result. Much greater co-ordination is required – although cohesion is difficult to achieve in practice. Four initiatives are required.

135. **First** the central role of the parent must be supported. If they are to feel in control of their often stressful situations, parents should have better access to information. They should be helped to understand and use it to support their child and seek the help that they need. Leaflets and pre-packaged sets of information are helpful, as are helplines to which parents can turn. Authorities without them should introduce them – piloting them initially if necessary. Parents should also be given access to all reports and letters written about their child and be involved in the planning of care. The Commission's survey indicated that lack of informaion was a problematic area, and anecdotal evidence suggests that the sharing of such information is appreciated and does no harm.

136. Medical support also needs to be co-ordinated. Given the prevalence of childhood disability, even a large GP practice with four or five partners is unlikely to have a new baby with Downs syndrome more than once in every eight to ten years; cerebral palsy will occur slightly less frequently as will some other impairments. It is unrealistic to expect GPs to be experts in childhood disability. It is important, nevertheless, that they should recognise that there is a problem and work with community paediatricians or CMOs. Community paediatric staff are ideally placed to provide the necessary continuity and service co-ordination, particularly in the early years.

137. **Second**, a focal point is needed for joint assessment, and the delivery and review of care in a way that draws the relevant agencies, services and professions together. Child development centres (CDCs) can play this role for the younger child, provided they adopt a child-centred approach, recognise the central position of the parent, and accept models of service provision which go beyond narrow medical, social or educational divisions. All children should have access to a CDC. Parents appreciate a 'single front door', which provides a single point of entry for all services.

138. For the older child the framework is less certain. The school is the most obvious point of contact for the parent and provides the greatest influence on a child's development outside of the family. Yet it will mainly (and quite properly) be concerned with education and its hours of opening will be restricted to school hours. The Department for Education has issued consultative proposals for implementing the special education provisions of the *Education Act 1993*, involving health, social services and education.

139. **Third** a single person is required to co-ordinate care for an individual child and family. Various models are possible. Someone can act as a point of contact – often the case with some key worker arrangements. At the other extreme, where needs are complex, someone needs to help the parent and child articulate concern, provide information, understand what is happening, and obtain or provide help. Community paediatric staff might undertake such a role. There are examples in social services of care managers, similar to those in community care, who specialise in disability and who have small budgets. While these are all effective ways of co-ordinating services, the potential of care managers who command substantial budgets and who can operate across services is considerable and requires further research. Care managers might be drawn from a variety of professions. Arguments have been put forward for the social worker, the health visitor, the school nurse, the educational psychologist, and the paediatrician. Others will no doubt protest their suitability. What is clear is that all are candidates and all will have to go beyond their current professional role to act effectively as care managers.

140. **Fourth,** there should be joint policies, strategies and operational arrangements between agencies. This represents the biggest challenge. Each agency must nominate a person to sit on a strategic planning team for children with a disability. This person must be of sufficient seniority to make decisions on behalf of his or her agency. Joint funding should be used to break down barriers between agencies and disciplines and change current systems. This is ambitious. A good place to start is the provision of joint equipment budgets and shared respite care. Agencies should develop an effective register of disabled children together. Unless the system for supporting disabled children is approached in this radical way then experience suggests that their needs will not be met in a comprehensive and wholehearted fashion. At the very least aids and equipment should be provided jointly by both health and social services.

✳ ✳ ✳

141. Whilst joint working must be the aim, authorities must also develop their own agendas. The following sections describe firstly, the agenda for health commissioners, secondly the agenda for providers of community child health services and thirdly the agenda for local authorities.

AN AGENDA FOR HEALTH COMMISSIONERS

142. For years health professionals have been aware of advice to measure needs, target services and evaluate outcomes. However, little has been done in the field of community child health services. To follow such advice requires considerable effort to change traditional patterns of work, and takes time, resources and training. Without a sufficient incentive little is likely to alter except among small groups of enthusiasts with special interests.

143. Times have changed, however, and at least two incentives are now present. Firstly, the *NHS and Community Care Act* (Ref. 1) has separated the commissioning from the provision of services; and it has given commissioners the duty to assess the relative needs of their populations. Secondly, budgets are more constrained and it makes good sense for commissioners to be as clear as possible about the value of what they are buying. *Health of the Nation* targets and those in the documents produced by the Welsh Office (refs. 5 and 6) also provide encouragement to focus services and measure outcomes. Commissioners, however, must be encouraged to use their powers wisely. There are indications that some commissioners may make significant changes to community child health services without first determining the extent of need, the value of current provision or the impact of changes on complementary services provided by other agencies such as social services.

144. Definitions and measurements of relative need are likely to be fairly crude to begin with but should improve year by year as information gathering becomes more sophisticated and authorities learn from their experience. Immunisation and the pre-school surveillance programme should be relatively easy as coverage, normally, is intended to apply to the whole child population.

SURVEILLANCE AND IMMUNISATION

145. There is guidance from the Department of Health and Welsh Office on which immunisations to give - although commissioners need to have accurate data on the proportion administered by GPs as this will effect the number of child health clinics required. Research reflects scepticism on the value of some surveillance (Ref. 24) but there is guidance from the Department of Health on a core programme. In the absence of local evidence that more than this core should be carried out, commissioners should specify the minimum programme recommended by the guidance which is based on the second edition of *Health for All Children* (Ref. 15), as indeed, a number of health authorities are now doing. They should also ensure that the professionals involved are made aware of the specification.

146. Commissioners must begin to move from the traditional 'block contracts' to those which specify the health surveillance checks and other activity required. They should calculate the resources needed to deliver the programmes, monitor the extent of coverage attained and link contracts to the achievement of outcomes.

CHILD HEALTH CLINICS

147. Except for the 18 month check, health surveillance should normally take place in child health clinics within a GP practice or in the community. Clinics should have a clear purpose. The type provided should be based on the needs of the locality. In some areas commissioners should purchase clinics on the basis that the main focus is to provide the formal health surveillance programme, with children attending by appointment. Unless the layout permits good separation of functions, open clinics with many families present are unlikely to offer the right environment for effective and efficient surveillance procedures. However, child health clinics offering a more comprehensive, open access service are likely to be more appropriate for some areas - particularly inner cities where there is a high level of mobility and/or homelessness in the population and a high number of families not registered with GPs. Research indicates that in these situations significant numbers of problems come to light during non-routine visits initiated by parents, health visitors or GPs (Ref. 29), suggesting that it would be unwise to discourage open access in such localities. Other clinics are for secondary assessments following a referral after initial surveillance. This is an important function but a CMO linked to a GP practice in the community may provide a more appropriate model for further assessment in some areas than a centralised clinic.

148. Some mothers value child health clinics for support and social reasons. They provide a place where mothers - particularly those with first babies or those who might otherwise be isolated - can meet, weigh their babies and obtain advice and reassurance. Usually, a core group of mothers attends regularly, and some research suggests that families from specific housing areas attend most (Ref. 30). This may suggest a need for a different type of service and commissioners should consider whether traditional child health clinics remain the most appropriate means of providing this type of support. Drop-in facilities in key locations - as part of a family centre, for example provided jointly with social services - may be an effective alternative. Innovative, group, health promotional or support activities might then be offered, facilitated by health visitors, nursery nurses or other workers, but expensive medical cover might be unnecessary.

149. Health commissioners need to be sure that with the rapid growth in child health clinics provided in GP surgeries the number of clinics run by the community health unit is adjusted to take this growth into account. They need to work with FHSAs to ensure that the GP accreditation procedure is sufficiently rigorous to allow this adjustment to take place by specifying high standards of training and procedures that will encourage parents to choose to attend their GP practices. One authority visited by the study team had an agreement with the FHSA that GPs seeking accreditation had to agree to run their child health clinics on similar lines to the community clinics. Parents then signed an option to attend either GP-run or community unit clinics and were then discouraged from attending those for which they had not opted. In this way, after parents had made a choice, duplication was avoided, and community unit clinic sessions were reduced as attendance levels declined. Whether or not health authorities are working successfully with FHSAs on this issue the attendance levels at their clinics should be monitored and clinics rationalised when consistently low attendance rates are registered at the same time as good overall coverage rates on the formal health surveillance programme.

150. FHSAs must also ensure that standards of GP clinics are maintained. At present there is little evaluation of the quality of GP work and there is a need to monitor much more rigorously than at present the child surveillance work undertaken by them. Whilst GPs cannot be removed formally from the list of those accredited, FHSAs have other management methods to ensure that standards are maintained. Child health surveillance is a clinical activity which should be audited, and conducted in appropriate environments with appropriately trained staff. Health commissioners can help to raise standards by specifying that there should be district co-ordinators – especially for hearing and sight tests - responsible for ensuring maximum coverage at the appropriate age, that tests are conducted effectively and efficiently and that subsequent, appropriate action is timely.

GP Fundholders

151. To ensure a coherent approach, which is still responsive to local needs, GP fundholders are an increasingly important group of health commissioners. They should be engaged with other commissioners as full and active participants in the development of a child health strategy based on health needs. The NHS Executive is expected to provide guidance on the need for collaboration by fundholders with the district health authority. FHSAs should strongly encourage GPs to reflect this strategic direction in their practice. To minimise the risk of GP fundholders developing their own approach in isolation, commissioners should work with them, so that commissioning decisions can be seen to reflect their views, and be responsive to changes in local need. At an operational level, an effective accreditation process should ensure that GPs are

providing a comparable service, which offers a real choice for parents, and which enables community services to be adjusted as GP activity increases. Simple information should be required by the FHSA (and in future by the merged DHA/FHSA commissioning authority), which is useful for clinical audit, and which is fed back to the practice, suitably anonymised, to allow GPs to compare their performance with that of others.

152. Health commissioners must also review and decide how the public health functions of health visiting are to be provided as GP fundholders cannot purchase this element of community nursing.

SCHOOL HEALTH

153. Health commissioners are obliged to contract for a school health service under statute but there is no specification of what should be done. The study team found the service under review at half the authorities visited – although without much consultation with the parents, children and schools involved. Before redefining the service in future contract specifications, purchasers should require a review – if one has not already been carried out. As part of this review, commissioners should seek the view of the parents, children, schools and the local education authority (LEA). Reviews should provide information on the structure, process and – if possible – outcomes of the current service and take account of population needs with consideration given to possibilities for substitution of tasks between different practitioners.

Exhibit 25
STAFFING OF SCHOOL HEALTH SERVICES
Local review should include levels of staffing and skill-mix

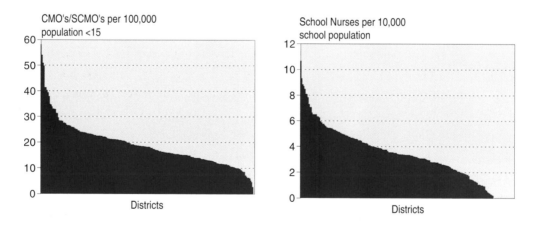

Source: Health Service Indicators 1990/1 and Welsh Office.

154. Programmes for surveillance for school age children have not been set out in government guidance. One activity that will need careful consideration is the school entry medical examination. In general, universal examinations should be dropped in favour of a selective approach – as is happening in many areas. It may be wise, however, following an assessment of population needs, for certain schools to be targeted for continuing universal medical examinations. Such schools are likely to be in areas of high deprivation and high population mobility - especially where they cater for significant numbers of service children or those from abroad. Commissioners will need to allow for this in their specifications, subject to clinical audit, taking account of findings from the pre-school checks.

155. The changing demography of the school population over the years is altering the importance of various school health functions. The school nurse is increasingly becoming the key professional involved. Commissioners should encourage this trend where appropriate - for example, by decreasing the involvement of doctors as school nurses become competent at administering immunisations. There may be certain schools that still require a greater involvement by doctors because of the number of pupils with special needs or the deprivation or high mobility of the children in their catchment areas. Child protection is an increasingly important topic for the school health service. School nurses must have adequate training in this area. The growing numbers of children with special needs in ordinary schools also means that the school health and general practice increasingly overlap – for example, in the management of asthma. School nursing and general practices must work closely together to plan services and provide each other with appropriate information. In recognition of the changing role of the school health service the British Paediatric Association has produced a discussion document to further the debate (Ref. 31).

156. Health education and health promotion are areas that are being developed. School nurses may be in a good position to provide both support and advice for teachers and counselling for pupils either individually or in groups. However, commissioners must be aware that a high degree of professionalism is required for this function which, as with health visiting, should be based on an assessment of needs. They must also require evaluation of the effectiveness and outcomes of this work and elicit the view of the parents, children and schools involved.

MONITORING AND EVALUATION

157. Commissioners require information, both to evaluate the effectiveness of activities purchased and to monitor the progress of the contract. Such information is lacking at present. The providers of service, although without much useful information themselves, have experience and are still in control, setting the agenda for contracts. The process should become one of dialogue, with each party sharing the information it possesses, to create a picture of needs, processes and outcomes. Commissioners must eventually require service providers to put forward proposals that maximise health gain, backed up by evidence of agreed needs, anticipated and actual outcomes and methods for evaluation. This approach will take time to develop. Authorities should not wait, however, for the perfect computer system. The community unit visited by the study team that was most advanced in changing health visiting practice from traditional patterns to one of maximising health gains by focusing work on targeted needs was monitoring this change, and shifting resources accordingly, by the use of manual systems supported by clinical audit. The information gathered was shared with commissioners.

158. To begin with, commissioners require information on the structure and the current pattern and method of provision. Apart from the proportion of children immunised, there is likely to be little information available on outcomes. Commissioners should start agreeing protocols for elements of the service with outcome indicators specified. They should also set out the form in which community trusts and units should notify them of progress. In one authority visited, commissioners were specifying that services should be targeted; the community trust was still continuing with blanket coverage but the commissioner had no way of knowing. The activity indicators specified should not be Korner contact data, which are of little operational use.

159. Outcome indicators (or suitable process indicators as a proxy) should clearly reflect the purpose of the activity and be relatively cheap to collect. The British Paediatric Association has identified some simple outcome measures for certain elements of child health and for the surveillance programmes in particular (Ref. 32). These should be used in setting goals supported by a rolling programme of individual case-by-case audit.

AN AGENDA FOR PROVIDERS OF COMMUNITY CHILD HEALTH

160. To a great extent issues for providers of community child health services mirror those for commissioners. Commissioners will begin – and have already begun in some places – to ask awkward questions about the health gain achieved by the services expenditure. Providers must prepare themselves to give adequate answers or face the prospect of arbitrary, and possibly unpalatable, reductions. Unfortunately, community health suffers from being the unglamorous section of the NHS, competing for resources with 'high-tech' acute hospitals. The community child health service must be able to demonstrate value for money by knowing the answers to the following:

— What do health visitors, medical officers and school nurses do?

— What are the demonstrated benefits arising from their activity?

— What are the health needs of the population?

— What priorities and criteria are being adopted?

— What skills are required to perform those functions?

— What information is required to monitor performance?

— How should the service be organised?

The first two questions were considered in chapter two; the other five are discussed below.

WHAT ARE THE HEALTH NEEDS OF THE POPULATION?

161. If commissioners are not already working with providers of community health services to assess local needs, then providers should not wait but instead should take the initiative themselves. The same demographic information is available to both and use should be made of the health visitors' and school nurses' knowledge of their patch or caseload. GP practice profiles, where they have been developed beyond basic lists of age and gender, can also be useful. The community child health service should aim to reach a consensus with GPs on the needs, priorities and the functions to be provided. At one unit visited the consultant community paediatrician had visited each GP practice within the district and successfully involved them in the shaping of the aims and direction of the community child health service.

162. Health visitors and school nurses should already be developing 'profiles' of their caseloads, to comply with their professional standards . In practice, they may need extra training and assistance to help them to do so. Profiles should reflect the relative needs and priorities agreed with the commissioners as part of the child health strategy and business plans. They should help to inform commissioners' decisions about the priorities to be addressed in the locality.

WHAT PRIORITIES AND CRITERIA ARE BEING ADOPTED?

163. If community child health services are to be effective, they will need priorities and criteria and will need to ensure that they are being addressed appropriately and in a consistent manner. It might take time to adjust to new working patterns. To promote ownership, professional groups should be involved in developing criteria. Training and advice will be needed. It has taken one community health trust five years to change its pattern of work, with routine work minimised and resources released for greater targeting (Case Study 3). It has taken time both to convince staff that changing from a traditional service pattern to a more focused approach based on assessment of needs and criteria is appropriate, and to determine the criteria to be used.

Case Study No. 3

**PRE-SCHOOL AGE COMMUNITY CHILD HEALTH SERVICES
IN NOTTINGHAM COMMUNITY HEALTH NHS TRUST**

ROUTINE WORK HAS BEEN MINIMISED AND RESOURCES RELEASED
FOR GREATER TARGETING

— Objective categories of need have been agreed by health visitor managers.

— All cases held by health visitors are classified according to category of 'need'.

— Cases are then deemed in need of 'high', 'medium' or 'low' levels of intervention.

— Classification of cases and the subsequent interventions by health visitors are reviewed with practitioners and managers, for appropriateness.

— Information from this system is used by managers to switch resources between localities, to match resources to needs.

— Traditional 'case-count' methods of workload management are not used.

WHAT SKILLS ARE REQUIRED?

164. Traditionally, community child health services have been specified in terms of staff roles and contact numbers - descriptions of services rather than of needs. Providers of community child health services must re-focus on needs and on the functions and skills required to meet them. As a result, there may need to be some adjustment to skill mix. It is important, that any such adjustment is based on needs and not on an arbitrary decision simply to reduce costs.

165. The role of clinical medical officers (CMOs) is changing. Many have acquired considerable experience in community child health without necessarily obtaining formal qualifications. Recognising this, the report of a joint working party on medical services for children (Ref. 33) recommended that the SCMO and CMO grades be integrated into the mainstream medical career structure within a combined child health service. It envisages that more of the medical input to community child health be delivered by doctors in training grades, although some career grade posts below consultant will continue to be required for the foreseeable future. The report also recommends that appointments to the SCMO and CMO grades cease. Duties appropriate to the career grade doctors include the provision of support to social services in fostering and adoption work and to education in statements of special needs. Providers should ensure that their use of these staff is determined by need and takes account of the growing involvement of other doctors - trainees in paediatrics and GPs – in these areas.

166. Health visiting and school nursing are other areas requiring skill-mix reviews. The study team found nursery nurses and health care assistants effectively being used together with the traditional grades. In one authority, health visitors had initiated their own skill mix review and, as a result, had reduced their numbers in a 'patch' team by a third and replaced them with qualified nursery nurses, a clinic co-ordinator and clerical staff. Nursery nurses, trained to recognise normal child development, undertook most of the non-medical aspects of the child health surveillance programme. They also provided intensive support, where needs had been identified through assessments by health visitors. All districts in Wales have undertaken skill mix reviews resulting in adjustments.

167. Staff should be adequately trained (and updated), – particularly when undertaking screening tests. Research has indicated that orthoptists are most effective for sight tests performed when children are aged three (Ref. 34). As a result in Northumberland Community Health NHS Trust these tests are undertaken by orthoptists.

WHAT INFORMATION IS REQUIRED?

168. Effective information systems are required for all the key activities undertaken by community child health services. For example, the coverage and referral rates on all surveillance processes should be accurately recorded and compared with numbers known to be in target populations. Details of clinic usage should be recorded. Where selective surveillance is being undertaken - e.g. at school entrance, coverage and referrals should be monitored. Referrals above specific ages for conditions such as sensorineural deafness, phenylketonuria and squint should be recorded with reasons for late referral. It is most important that the results of recording are fed back to the staff involved for self-audit and to managers to enable them to monitor the effectiveness of screening programmes and the efficiency with which procedures are operated. The appointment of co-ordinators for key areas such as sight and hearing can also help. As a result of a systematic approach to surveillance and simple, but effective, information systems Dr Allan Colver reports in research on evaluation of the health surveillance of pre-school children (Ref. 35) that over a six year period of research in Northumberland, significant improvements in the processes and outcomes have been achieved (case study 4).

HOW SHOULD THE SERVICE BE ORGANISED?

169. The British Paediatric Association recommends that the child health services should be led by a consultant paediatrician and that community and acute sectors should eventually be combined to provide a seamless service for patients and their families. The Commission has stated its support for this objective in a previous report (Ref. 7). In community health services, a consultant community paediatrician can bring the benefits of increased status for the service and added drive towards quality and evaluation. Most children rarely need acute in-patient care but virtually all children use community child health services.

Case Study 4

EVALUATION OF THE HEALTH SURVEILLANCE OF PRE-SCHOOL CHILDREN IN NORTHUMBERLAND.

SIGNIFICANT IMPROVEMENTS HAVE BEEN ACHIEVED.

— The immunisation cover for measles has risen from 58% to 96%, for diphtheria, tetanus, and for polio from 78% to 97% and for pertussis from 30% to 91%.

— The screening test cover has risen for 6 week tests from 79% to 96%, for 8 month tests from 80% to 90% and for 3 year tests from 79% to 88%.

— The median age at which deafness greater than 60 decibels is recognised has fallen from 18 to 9 months. The proportion of deaf children recognised after age 12 months has fallen from 55% to 37%.

— The median age at which cerebral palsy is recognised has fallen from 7 to 4 months for quadriplegia and from 9.5 to 7 months for hemiplegia. The upper quartile age has fallen from 10 to 7 months for quadriplegia and from 25 to 10 months for hemiplegia.

— The median age at referral for speech therapy for language disorder needing special educational provision has fallen from 40 to 28 months. The proportion of such children recognised after age 3 years has fallen from 56% to 16%.

— The proportion of boys undergoing orchidopexy for cryptorchidism before age 6 years has risen from 18% to 42%. [An operation to fix the testis in the scrotum, done in certain cases of undescended testis].

Source: Dr Allan Colver

170. The Cumberledge Report (Ref. 36) argued for 'patch-based' health visiting with a discrete geographical area or 'patch' served by a single health visitor or team. The trend, however, which is recognised by the Department of Health (Ref. 37), has been for health visitors to be 'attached' to GP practices, serving the needs of the patients on GPs' lists. As GP practices overlap, so too do different attached health visitor teams. Most health visitors are now organised on this basis, which is highly appropriate in areas where need amounts to little more than new baby visits, immunisation and surveillance, or where practices equate with geographical areas as may happen in some rural locations. However, it may not be the most cost-effective method of delivering all services to all families. There are some services which may be organised more appropriately within geographical areas rather than to the dispersed populations on a GP's list. In areas where needs are high, and concentrated, some 'patch-work' is desirable. It is probably essential where there are significant members of people from ethnic minorities, and health visitors require specialist knowledge of languages and cultures to be effective. Patch working also facilitates joint work with agencies such as social services, especially where families and children within a community are offered support through a family centre.

171. Three important factors affect the balance between these two approaches:

— **the size of practice population:** attached work can be impractical and inefficient in small practices – especially in single-handed practices.

NHS   SSD

— **the distribution of needs within the child population:** in areas of high need certain functions can be organised more effectively on a patch basis, such as group work in a deprived housing area. Some more intensive work may also be organised more cost-effectively on a patch basis when several neighbours living close to one another require similar support or special skills. Whole housing estates, blocks of flats or streets may need targeting for support work (in conjunction with social services authorities). It makes little sense to work in a fractured and uncoordinated way from several GP practices. Most good health visiting seen by the study team (which involved focused work and a balanced skill mix) was patch-based. One authority, however, mixed the two approaches working on an 'attached' basis except in a highly deprived area of the district, where the 'public health' activities, including group work, were detached from the GP practice health visitors and addressed separately – realising the best of both worlds.

— **the degree of interest of GPs in preventive work with children who are not ill** was considered by the professionals involved to be of critical importance to successful outcomes. Where GPs take a keen interest, practice based work is effective; where they do not, patch-based work may be more successful.

172. In deciding whether to operate on an attached or a patch basis providers of community health services should take account of arrangements in GP practices. Where needs are low, or where a GP practice population more or less equates with the geographical population, then attached working should operate well. In inner city (or other) areas with single handed GPs, high numbers of people from ethnic minorities and high need, patch working is likely to be more cost-effective. For areas which are mixed, or lie in between these two extremes, a combination of patch working for group activities and other public health functions, and attached work for formal surveillance and individual contacts may be appropriate. Other factors which must also be taken into account in deciding how to organise services are the distribution of GP fundholders (who may in any case dictate their requirements), and the local arrangements in other agencies – particularly social services.

AN AGENDA FOR SOCIAL SERVICES FOR CHILDREN

173. The Children Act presents social services authorities with demanding challenges, similar to those for adult services resulting from the NHS and Community Care Act. It places a strong emphasis on the assessment of needs, both strategic and individual, and requires packages of care to be tailored to meet individual needs. Significant changes in approach are required to focus on needs rather than services, to achieve more corporate action and to secure closer collaboration with parents and other agencies. The Criminal Justice Act 1991 also requires changes, and with three such major pieces of legislation to implement, social services authorities are under pressure, particularly as many of them are also being asked to make cuts in their current and planned budgets.

174. This section outlines some strategic actions that authorities can take. They must start by assessing needs which will then inform the joint assessment of children in need. Social services should also review current patterns of service and field social work to identify ways of freeing resources for reinvestment. They must then reshape services as necessary to ensure they meet the assessed needs of children.

REVIEWING SERVICES AND COSTS

175. Authorities should review current services, their costs, quality, organisation, and pattern of use to see if there is any mismatch, and any scope to release resources for re-investment elsewhere. Services should be seen on a continuum, supporting a range of needs. The mix is important as it can affect the benefit of the service to the child and the cost to the authority. Most authorities visited had reviewed, or were in the process of reviewing, elements of their services; but parts of the service should not be looked at in isolation, as performance in one can have an impact upon others. Organisation and management of residential care staff and the support of foster carers should be looked at in order to determine how to ensure these services provide the best possible care for children. The needs of children already supported by social services should be included in the review, not only to help assess the quality of the support provided to them but also to gauge whether another service would be more appropriate. Is a child in a residential home because of a shortage of foster places? (If so, why is there a shortage?) Is a child being looked after away from home because of a lack of a specific support service?

176. Two other considerations are important in any review of costs. Firstly, social services departments are not wholly in command of their budgets. The courts can, and do, order a child to be provided with a specific form of care financed by the local authority. This care may well be expensive. Secondly, service costs available to senior management are currently calculated in a crude fashion and do not reflect accurately the total cost of a package of care provided for a child. Expenditure is service-based not child-based.

REVIEWING FIELD SOCIAL WORK PRACTICE AND ORGANISATION

177. A review of field social work practice and organisation should be integral to any review of services. Social workers make important decisions about assessment and service provision. Strategic decisions on the balance of services, who they serve and how they operate, cannot sensibly be taken without taking into account the role of social workers. Field social workers are also a significant resource in their own right and management should know what they do on a day-by-day basis.

178. In addition, because of their pivotal role, social workers need to be among the first to embrace the change in approach introduced by the Children Act. Their working practices should reflect this approach, although they work in a climate at least partially created for them by the political and administrative structures within which they work.

179. Their major area of work is undoubtedly child protection. Lack of information means it is impossible to say with certainty the amount of time spent on this activity but research (Ref. 22) and anecdotal evidence from authorities visited suggest it is very high. Descriptions such as 'overwhelmed' and 'over burdened' are used and little time appears to be available for what is regarded as less crisis-driven work including the provision of support for 'children in need'. This raises five issues that should be included in a review of social work.

1. **Workload management and social work supervision.** A social worker may feel overburdened because of inadequate workload management or insufficient supervision and support. Both are essential for good social work practice. The quality of practice must be audited by professionals during the review. What does a social worker do during contact with families and children? Are social workers listening to parents and

children and working more in partnership with them? What practice standards are there and how can the quality of practice be monitored most effectively? Pressure can be reduced if good management reveals inefficient practice that can be discontinued.

2.   **The spread of resources between teams.**   If there is an inadequate workload management system, senior managers may not be accurately informed of the levels of different work undertaken by different areas or teams of field social workers. As a result the amount, or distribution of resources between teams may be out of balance.

3.   **Social workers' response to 'child protection' referrals.**   As indicated in chapter two, research suggests that only some 15% of all such referrals lead to registration and two thirds of the cases investigated after an initial filter may not result in a case conference at which registration is considered (Ref. 22). Such figures suggest that an initial response other than a full child protection investigation may be more appropriate in many cases. Guidelines for social workers on child protection referrals should be examined. What risk indicators are used and could assessment for another form of support be more appropriate in some cases? Answering these questions will require better information on referrals and their outcomes.

4.   **The impact of too little available time.**   The needs of children and families other than those involved in child protection may not be met properly and the quality of assessments and support provided may be poor if social workers have insufficient time. For instance, is a child placed in residential care as an 'emergency' because it is quicker and simpler than undertaking a more thorough assessment and organising services to support the child and family at home? Are children who 'leave care' drifting for want of sufficient time and attention from social workers?

5.   **Social workers' attitude(s) to 'children in need'.**   Although policy statements indicate a range of children in need – from children suffering abuse or neglect to less critical concerns – as highlighted in chapter two, it was apparent both from authority visits and research that social workers still regard 'children in need' as a separate category of children with a low priority rather than all children with whom they work. Many social workers have not yet made the intellectual shift away from categorising children according to services. Research suggests this may be why nearly half of child protection cases which did not reach a case conference received no services for support either (Ref. 22). Health visitors interviewed by the study team were concerned that children referred by them to social services were not getting any support.

The social work duty system for receiving child care referrals should also be included in the review, together with the level and range of clerical and administrative tasks.

REVIEWING RESIDENTIAL CARE

180. The most frequent obstacle to change cited to the study team was a lack of resources with which to develop new services. Many authorities, however, still have a major resource which could be unlocked for this purpose. Residential care is the most expensive form of support used (see Chapter One) and concern has been expressed nationally about its quality (Refs. 26 and 38). As a result, a residential care support force has been set up by the Department of Health to help authorities to make improvements. Residential care has decreased in volume since 1981, as a significant number of authorities have closed homes, but some authorities could reduce it still further in favour of foster care - although it is important to retain some provision as an essential option for certain children.

181. If all authorities were to achieve the mix of services adopted by the authorities making greatest use of fostering in England (excluding authorities that have removed their own residential provision completely), the Commission estimates that up to £100 million might be released (Appendix 1). It is important, however, that any alternative form of care is of good quality and appropriate to the individual children involved. A child is unlikely to benefit from foster care, for example, if he or she experiences multiple placement breakdowns.

182. It would be extremely naive to assume that reductions could be made automatically. In some situations, savings can no doubt be made without too much difficulty where there is already significant spare capacity allowing closure of an existing home. At least two authorities visited during the study believed this to be possible in their areas, releasing staff for other duties such as outreach work. In other authorities some of the funds released would be needed to reinvest in other homes to improve staffing levels, grades and training. A reduction in residential care could also require more support for foster carers, as problems presented by the children they foster increase in complexity as a result.

183. So while there appears to be scope for considerable savings and reinvestment, it is important to proceed with caution if such opportunities are to be realised in a constructive and positive way without jeopardising quality of care or putting staff morale at risk. Any changes must be managed with great care and skill.

184. **In summary,** if social services are to match services to needs in a cost effective way and encourage the cultural shift required in the Children Act, certain first steps should be adopted. The extent of relative needs within the population must be assessed and priorities defined in accordance with budgetary limitations. The organisation, costs, quality, effectiveness and inter-relationships between different elements of services currently provided should be reviewed. As part of this review, the organisation and working practices of field social workers should also be assessed. Following these reviews the social services authority should be better placed to take strategic decisions on the balance of resources required between different geographical areas and competing needs, on possible models for organising and delivering services, and on management information required to monitor outcomes.

185. All of this activity suggests a need for someone to co-ordinate these initiatives. An individual (or individuals) should be nominated to undertake this role. Without such co-ordi-nation, improvements are unlikely to occur and social services authorities' new responsibilities under the Children Act are unlikely to be fulfilled.

SETTING A NEW COURSE IN SOCIAL SERVICES

186. Reviews of needs and services must then lead to a revision of social services activity. The Children Act sets the agenda: to protect children from significant harm and, in partnership with parents and other agencies, to safeguard and promote their health and development. The strategies that authorities develop should translate these broad objectives into a balanced range

SSD

of activities. As chapter two has demonstrated, service inputs have been measured in the past rather than outcomes for the children and families involved. Senior management must have a clear vision of what services are to achieve in terms of these outcomes. Staff at all levels must be equally clear what outcomes are expected at operational and individual case levels. Knowledge of achievement – or otherwise – is obviously vital. This requires the collection and analysis of information which must then be used as a management tool to review and adjust service activity accordingly.

IMPROVING INFORMATION SYSTEMS

187. Once information is available, new strategies can be developed, re-organisation set in train and pilot projects assessed. Information systems which provide feedback on current activity come first. They can take a manual form, initially, or perhaps be developed on personal computers. Information gathered on current activity can help feed the review process and the consequent development of strategy and service models. It will also provide a database from which to measure the extent of change and improvement when new strategies are implemented.

188. Both activity and financial information in the past have concentrated on service usage rather than service outcomes, encouraged by government statistical requirements. This type of information still has its uses but they are limited. To ensure services become responsive to needs and deliver desired outcomes, the experiences and careers of individual children within the system must be capable of analysis and aggregation. Financial information must also become more sophisticated so that it becomes possible to cost the support given to an individual child or family. No authority visited had comprehensive management information of this type. A number had made a useful start, however, and new Department of Health returns should help to address some of the deficiencies.

— Oxfordshire and Cheshire social services departments were using a simple method to monitor child protection referrals by area teams. This allows referrals to be tracked through a filtering system to case conference and registration. Both workloads and significant variations in filtering between area teams are monitored. Where necessary, individual cases are reviewed to verify the appropriateness of decisions. (This system might be extended to record the number of referrals not reaching case conference but diverted to some form of support service.)

— The leaving care officer at one authority was able to tell the study team the circumstances in which all his young people were living: by category of accommodation, by main income source and by main occupation. A second authority was also able to provide significant information on care leavers through a one-off review to assess their needs.

— The fostering and adoption officer at another authority kept a manual record showing where individual children were fostered relative to their own homes, the dates that foster care had begun and terminated and the reason for termination (whether planned or unplanned). These records were used to spot problems within the service resulting in placement breakdown and to recruit appropriate carers located where and when needed.

— Oxfordshire social services were also able to track the careers of children looked after using a computer programme. This system allows field social work teams and senior managers to monitor the movements in and out of the 'looked after' system, the legal status of children and the reasons for entering and leaving accommodation (including whether there are any planned objectives). Reports are received quarterly and variations between teams and over time can be monitored.

FIELD SOCIAL WORK
The role of field social workers

189. Field social workers specialised in child care work in all social services authorities visited except one. The highly specialised demands of the NHS and Community Care Act and the Children Act among others indicate that generic working across client groups is unlikely to be feasible. The question is whether even greater specialisation is desirable, in particular for child protection work, adolescents and children with a disability. Although the answer is likely to be yes, it is not without problems. There is a perceived 'elitism' in protection work, and specialisation can de-skill non-child protection workers at the same time as locking specialists into a narrow band of responses during investigations. On the other hand, the increased knowledge, confidence and support that specialising brings reduces 'burn-out'. One or two authorities visited were beginning to specialise (case study 5, overleaf), and were concluding that whilst philosophically such a move is hard, pragmatically it is the way forward if social work is to be efficiently provided and cost effective. Work is focused and of a high standard, individual strengths of social workers are harnessed, and staff resources are released for non-child protection work.

190. Apart from child protection work, two other areas emerged from this study as contenders for specialisation. The first was work with adolescents (which might well involve protection) and the second was care management for children with disabilities. Adolescents have specific needs. The opinions of young people who talked to the study team strongly suggest that both the attention given to adolescents and the outcomes are improved by specialising. The requirements of children with a disability are so complex, as already described, that specialisation is necessary to ensure that such children and their families get the best advice and support possible.

61

Case Study 5
ONE OR TWO AUTHORITIES HAD DEVELOPED
SPECIALISED FIELD SOCIAL WORK

CHESHIRE SOCIAL SERVICES

— District office within county. Represents northern industrial city, population serviced: 200,000 (46,400 children aged under 18).

— Referrals arrive at Customer Reception (generic social services) permanently staffed by three social workers, three receptionists, a community care worker, a team leader and the service manager.

— 24 hour turn-round on referrals by Customer Reception. If the section cannot resolve the referral by their own actions within this time the referral will be given a priority rating and passed to a specialist team.

— The seven priority levels for action are standard throughout authority. Audit held by social services to ensure they are applied consistently across authority.

— Specialist children's support teams:

1. **Child protection** (includes seconded health visitor)
    Advantages: team members' confidence and ability increases with development of specialist knowledge and experience. 'Burn-out' decreases. Support valued between team members who share similar experiences and knowledge.
    Disadvantages: de-skills other social workers – danger they will not recognise child protection issues within their own cases. Child protection team members not introduced to alternative approaches in how they handle referrals for potential child protection.
    Future development: addressing de-skilling problem by co-working child protection investigations, with a member from the child protection team working with a social worker from another children's team.

2. **Family Support** (two teams) for children aged under eight, working from family centres – concentrate on pro-active support for families and children in need. Developing innovative, flexible responses to needs. Each team has freedom to spend £1,000 per annum sec. 17 money. Other sec. 17 money can be applied for.

3. **Over-Eights Family Team** – concentrates mainly on children aged 8 to 15 who are living at home with their families.

4. **Placement Team** – supports children in residential and foster care

5. **Adolescent Resource Team** – concentrates on adolescents aged 15 and over, including youth justice.

6. **Special Needs Team** – concentrates on children with disabilities and their families.

In addition there is a specialist team to recruit and support foster carers.

SSD

Sharpening procedures for assessments and care planning

191. The understandable concerns about child protection and the consequent detailed guidance from the Department of Health have ensured that assessment procedures are more disciplined and rigorous. A similar discipline should become the norm for children with other needs. Strategic guidance is required on the form assessments should take and the circumstances under which they should be carried out. At present, some social workers wish to undertake full assessments on every occasion, when a lesser response might do. On the other hand, assessments can be inadequate because of a lack of guidance on procedures and processes. The Department of Health has issued recommended standard screening and assessment tools for children considered for residential or foster care which have been developed by Roy Parker et al (Ref. 25). They are thorough – and make the essential links between assessment, planning, service provision and outcomes. Authorities that have used this tool have been enthusiastic - as have foster carers.

192. Assessment of children's needs should be linked in this way to the process of care planning and to the assessment of outcome. Care planning for children on the protection register is done in a multi-agency forum (although it is not as good as it could be – the emphasis is mostly on assessment as opposed to the resulting care plan). A multi-disciplinary approach should be adopted in planning care for other children such as those being 'looked after'. Day and residential care managers and fostering officers are experts in their own spheres and should be involved in the planning process. Other specialists, such as psychologists, health visitors and representatives from education may also need to contribute. The gatekeeping procedure for residential and foster care proved to be a key element in the link between assessment and service provision authorities visited.

Making better use of the staff through workload management

193. It is important that the workloads of field social workers should be properly managed to ensure that priorities are met, that social workers are not overburdened and that resources are matched to areas of need. A workload management system should be introduced that:

— is consistent throughout the department

— prioritises work

— takes account of workers' experience

— provides feedback to first line managers

— provides aggregated information to senior management

In addition to a formal workload management system, the quality of social work should be monitored. This will require a method of inspection and quality assurance. For example, team leaders (and senior managers) can accompany social workers on selected case visits. A model of peer review of cases - akin to medical audit – can be developed, and the assessment tools described above can also be used in evaluating the quality of social work.

SSD

CHILDREN LOOKED AFTER

Improving the management of services for children who are looked after

194. Fostering and residential care should be seen as part of a spectrum of accommodation provided for children looked after. Residential care should not be regarded as 'the last resort' when all else fails nor should it merely be an option. It should have a clearly defined purpose and ethos offering specific support for specific needs. Each residential home and fostering scheme should be clear about its purpose and its aims for the children and young people it looks after.

195. From the range of fostering arrangements observed by the study team the important features of an effective service can be summarised as:

— regular information on the precise needs of children requiring placements;

— a recruitment process geared to precise needs (if necessary, those of individual children);

— an agreement on the aims and outcomes of each placement;

— monitoring of outcomes and changing needs;

— support and training of foster carers to equip them for their tasks.

196. Good support and training of foster carers is essential. Their absence, more than that of any other feature (including payment levels) appears to adversely affect the recruitment, retention and quality of carers. Authorities aiming to reduce residential care will need to pay particular attention to these aspects. From information at authorities, twenty carers (including couples) or less is likely to be the maximum number that can be supported adequately by one fostering officer. This was the average number in the authorities visited where fostering schemes had the key features described in the previous paragraph. For highly specialised schemes such as remand fostering, greater support (and fewer carers per support officer) may be necessary.

197. To be successful, fostering and adoption should be managed as a service with specialist officers. Field social workers engaged in child care should not be required to recruit and support foster carers and undertake adoption work. There should be a central point from which information on foster care vacancies and their characteristics can be obtained by social workers.

198. Residential care requires good management. The features that are important include clear aims and objectives, criteria for referral, thorough assessments and care planning and regular monitoring of progress (Case Study 6). Children should also be consulted. At one authority visited, when three homes were closed and replaced by one new home, the children involved were consulted about the design of the new home. When possible properties were identified, a small group of the children viewed each one. Their choice was eventually developed as the new home.

199. It is essential that staffing levels are sufficient for the tasks in hand. The *Pindown Experience and the Protection of Children* (Ref. 26) stated that no member of staff, however well qualified or experienced, should be on duty alone with children. On the basis that five staff members are required to provide one member on duty 24 hours a day and that at least two staff should be present when children are at home, a minimum of eight or nine people are likely to be required to staff even the smallest home with the easiest tasks. With more young people, or children with greater problems, staff numbers should be higher. Young people who are unemployed or not at school - an increasing problem - may require more staff to be on duty during the

Case Study 6

IMPORTANT ELEMENTS OF A RESIDENTIAL SERVICE

(as illustrated by the Strategy for Challenging Behaviour – South Glamorgan County Council).

— Principles/standards underpinning the Strategy are written down.

— General aims and detailed objectives are set out in written guidance, e.g.

   — to work constructively with children aged 10 to 16 who display seriously challenging behaviour;

   — to ensure all alternative plans have been explored before removing a child from home;

   — to reduce or eliminate presenting behaviour problems.

— Criteria are laid down for referral to the scheme. (These were decided after reference to research and government guidelines.) Criteria to cover:

   — unsocialised behaviour

   — aggression and violence

   — inappropriate sexual behaviour

   — self abuse

   — substance abuse

   — firesetting
   (to assist potential referers a checklist is provided for each criterion)

— Referral route is set out in guidelines, together with form of assessment and who should do it (joint between referring agency/social services team, member of appropriate team operating the strategy team and the family), and the time scale for completion.

— Procedure is laid down in guidelines for a planning meeting to consider the assessment and the consequent objectives. Responsibility for chairing and minuting also set out. Objectives include e.g.

   — to accept/reject referral

   — to establish/review care plan

   — to match child's needs to resources

   — to make agreements with family

   — to allocate case accountability

   — to identify how/when plans will be reviewed

— Once child placed in home his/her progress against objectives of care plan is reviewed weekly with child.

— Placements are formally reviewed monthly to prevent 'drift'.

— Each home has a stated purpose and written procedural guidelines.

— Management structure and responsibilities are laid down.

Support structure in place, including: 24 hours community resource team to undertake assessments, support families and develop community resources; and an education liaison officer to facilitate a child's educational placement.

65

day. Residential staff look after increasingly damaged and difficult young people on a daily basis. They are responsible for their welfare, and are likely to be important contributors to any care plans. Their training and status needs to reflect the responsibilities and demands of their roles as residential social workers. Both need improvement as these staff have been under-valued. Specialist support from psychologists for residential (and foster) care workers can be of benefit in helping them to work with the challenges presented by the children and young people in their care. One authority has two psychologists, and staff find their skills helpful. The psychologists are currently evaluating their work. The need for improvements in the quality of residential care may well mean an investment in this type of service provision.

200. Admissions arrangements for residential care were considered important in every authority visited. In part, the focus was around the quality of assessments and care planning for individual children. The issue has broader implications, however, and a successful admission should take the following points into account:

— there should be explicit terms of reference for gatekeeping panels which make clear their role in the individual planning system;

— both the field social worker and residential or foster care worker and their managers need to feel responsible for the problems to be addressed in each case presented.

— workers who have skill in direct care and in foster care support should be represented in individual planning decisions;

— the arrangements for emergency placements should be integral to the system rather than a means of by-passing it.

201. Social services and education need to accept joint responsibility for the problem of disrupted education of children 'looked after' and should be working together to find solutions. At one authority visited, social services has appointed a qualified teacher as an 'education liaison officer'. The remit for the job is wide, encompassing 'any work that either supports a child's current educational placement or facilitates a return to appropriate schooling'. Liaising and building good relationships with schools are essential elements of the job, as are creating links with community based activities for children or young people such as youth projects and the Community Services Volunteers. The education liaison officer also offers support and encouragement to the children, for instance by trying to ensure that the right environment exists for homework. During 1991/92, this officer supported 34 children, only two of whom were still permanently excluded from school after her intervention. This illustration provides just one model for addressing the problems of disrupted education.

Helping young people leave care at age 16+

202. In a number of authorities, policies concerning young people leaving care were new or under development but there were examples of effective practice that had been developed over a longer period and that had had positive outcomes. Once again, clear structures, processes and purposes are important.

203. Leaving care divides into two parts: preparing a young person before they leave foster or residential care and helping them to adjust to independence or a return to their families once they have left. Preparations in advance should include:

— a procedure for preparing a leaving care plan for the young person at the age of 14 or 15;

— a system for ensuring that the planning took place;

— clarity over who is to co-ordinate the plan. (Residential or foster carers are in a position to take the lead. Field social workers' workloads and priorities are unlikely to allow them time to devote to this task. They also might not be the most competent persons to undertake them.)

204. Accommodation and a daytime occupation are major concerns for young people leaving care. An inter-agency approach to their concerns is therefore essential. Housing authorities, education and the voluntary sector should all be key players. In practice, young adults leaving care received the most effective support where agencies collaborated with each other. The reliability and amount of assistance available were specified in agreements between social services and housing authorities or associations. Good relations with education resulted in grants for further education and training. Leaving-care officers are needed who are pro-active, and who foster good relationships not only with the young people themselves but also with prospective employers and those who control access to housing and further education.

205. A separate structure for helping young people who have left care would appear to help them adjust to independence (Case Study 7). The ethos of social services child care is of caring for and supporting a child who is dependent. Having left care, young people need a different approach in order to learn to cope with being alone and to take responsibility for their own lives. A young person who has left care is also likely to reject social work - at least in the short term -

SSD

Case Study 7

SOCIAL SERVICES PROVISION FOR YOUNG PEOPLE LEAVING CARE

A SEPARATE STRUCTURE HELPS YOUNG PEOPLE ADJUST TO
INDEPENDENCE IN HAMMERSMITH AND FULHAM

Policy – The Independent Living Project (ILP) aims to enhance the life chances of young people who have been 'looked after', by helping them to prepare for independent living and integrate into the wider community.

The policy statement, which was agreed by both education and social services committees, was developed in consultation with young people who have been recipients of the service and with national consumer groups.

How it works – A 'landmark review' is undertaken with young people looked after between ages 14 and 15 to explore their needs in relation to the transition to independence. This will include life skills, education and training needs.

Everyone allocated a place at ILP will have a nominated key worker with whom to co-ordinate preparatory work with the young person and their social worker.

Young people leaving care between the ages of 17 and 21 years, who have been looked after for at least 12 months, are entitled to be nominated for local authority housing. A specific assessment will be carried out by a member of the ILP when the young person is aged 17. This assessment is presented to a housing panel and a decision is made about whether the young person is ready to take up a housing nomination.

While practical skills are important, the policy explicitly recognises the importance of other skills which are important in determining success after leaving care: the ability to negotiate, deal with conflict, recognise problems and know where to go for help in solving them.

— There is an agreement with the housing department for young people leaving care to receive priority for housing. This is not linked to a set age although a tenancy will not be given before age 18. The philosophy of the project is that independent living will only be successful if it is tailored to meet the needs of the young person - providing accommodation when young people are ready.

— In order to be nominated for a tenancy, the young person must have satisfied the ILP worker that they are able to cope. This is done by living in hostel / semi-independent accommodation until they are felt to be ready (usually around a year). This is provided in partnership with the voluntary sector. The young person must also satisfy certain requirements (ability to pay the rent, establish day time activities) in order to be considered suitable for a tenancy.

Nature of service – The ILP has its own identity, although part of the SSD, and the workers are clearly designated as leaving care workers and do not carry other responsibilities. A range of services is available at the centre or on an outreach basis for young people for whom the centre is inaccessible. These include:

— Reviews and planning meetings with the young people and others

— Advice, information and support facility according to the young person's needs via a 'duty system' or the young person's own key worker.

— Careers service outreach work

> **The ILP centre is available to young people for specific purposes. It is not available as a general social meeting place for young people.**
>
> The team consists of a team leader, an administrator and 5 workers.
>
> **Outcomes** – The ILP has been supporting young people leaving care since September 1987, since which time 94 young people have been housed, of which 3 tenancies have broken down. Rent and utility arrears are monitored.

and, (in the words of one young person) relate more positively to someone 'who's not like a social worker.'

✳ ✳ ✳

206. Whatever balance is decided between different needs and service elements it is important that the resulting structure produces a managed service. There must be clarity of purpose in process and outcome, clearly expressed and understood, at strategic, operational and individual case levels. Service provision is not an end in itself; it is there to promote positive outcomes for the children and families involved. Objectives should be set for processes and interim outcomes and performance should be regularly monitored through statutory and other reviews.

4. Summary of Recommendations

DEVELOPING JOINT PARTNERSHIPS

JOINT ASSESSMENT OF NEEDS AND DEVELOPMENT OF A STRATEGY

— Joint definition must be agreed of needs that can be met (para 109).

— Involvement of education and others such as voluntary bodies is important in developing a joint strategy published by health, social services and education authorities (para 110).

— Use should be made of OPCS and other demographic data to build up a picture of the incidence of risk indicators in a local area (para 111).

— Full commitment from the top of the organisation, and a corporate approach to developing the strategy is important (para 113).

— Parents are partners and should also be involved (para 114).

OPERATIONAL AREAS OF COMMON INTEREST

Family Support

— Good, written information for new parents should be provided and a contact point for further advice including an out-of-hours help-line (para 117).

— Contact by HV after a first visit to each family with a new baby should be based on assessed needs and agreed priorities (para 118).

— Any reduction in HV resources should take place only after a proper assessment and evaluation of current cover (para 119).

— Family centres could provide a focus for multi-agency community support for parents and children (para 120).

— Inclusion might be possible of some child development centre activities at appropriate family centres (para 121).

— HV activity in areas of high needs, and their public health and group work could be organised with advantage withs social services on a geographical basis (para 122).

— Distinction between roles of family centres and nurseries should be clear (para 123).

— A mixed system of open access with a quota of referred families is a preferred system for family centres where possible. Open drop-in facilities needed if centres are for referred families only (para 123).

— Voluntary organisations offering programmes of support to parents by parents can be cost-effective (para 125).

— DHAs should be prepared to allow funding for the design and evaluation of support programmes (para 126).

— After joint agreement on needs and priorities joint agreement on skill-mixes are required (para 127).

— A broader approach in social services should divert some families into universal provision but such approaches must be evaluated (para 128).

— A broader approach in social services will require a redirection of resources (para 129).

— A broader approach in social services will require an effective duty system, good training and clear procedures (para 130)

Child Protection

— Greater efforts are needed to develop good liaison with and co-operation of schools (para 132).

— Improvements needed in management information e.g. numbers of referrals, progress through investigation, services provided and outcome (para 133).

Support for Children with a Disability

— The central role of the parent must be supported with better information (para 135).

— Medical support needs to be co-ordinated (para 136).

— A focal point is needed for joint assessment. Child development centres provide this for pre-school children (para 137). Options should be explored for older children (para 138).

— A single person is required to co-ordinate care for an individual child and family (para 139).

— Agencies must act together jointly to produce strategies and operational agreements. Joint equipment budgets and shared respite care would be a good beginning (para 140).

AN AGENDA FOR HEALTH COMMISSIONERS
SURVEILLANCE AND IMMUNISATION

— Department of Health guidance on child health surveillance should be adopted by all health authorities unless there is contrary evidence. Authorities must ensure practitioners are aware of the policy (para 145).

— Commissioning authorities must move from 'block' contracts to those which specify the health surveillance checks and other activity required. Resources for these should be calculated and contracts linked to coverage and outcomes (para 146).

CHILD HEALTH CLINICS

— Type of clinic provided should be based on the assessed needs of the locality; some may be appointment-only for child health surveillance checks, others open-access for anyone (para 147).

— For some needs in some areas drop-in clinic facilities as part of a multi-agency family centre might be appropriate (para 148).

— Health commissioners should ensure that community run clinics are rationalised according to attendance and the growth of GP run clinics (para 149).

— FHSAs must ensure standards of GP clinics are maintained (para 150).

GP FUNDHOLDERS
— GP fundholders should be engaged with other commissioners in the development of child health strategies (para 151).

SCHOOL HEALTH
— Local reviews should be carried out of the current school health service unless this has been done. Parents, children and schools should be consulted (para 153).

— For many schools a universal school entry medical should be dropped in favour of a selective approach (para 154).

— The functions of the school health service should be clarified, with school nurses becoming the lead professional (para 155).

— Health commissioners must ensure school nurses are appropriately and effectively trained if they carry out health education or health promotion activities (para 156).

MONITORING AND EVALUATION
— Improved information systems and use of currently available information are required. The process should be a dialogue between commissioners and providers (paras 157-159).

AN AGENDA FOR PROVIDERS OF COMMUNITY CHILD HEALTH

WHAT ARE THE HEALTH NEEDS OF THE POPULATION?
— Providers should not wait if commissioners are not yet working with them to assess the local needs. Demographic information can be used together with practitioner information (para 161).

— Practitioners should continue to develop caseload profiles (para 162).

WHAT PRIORITIES AND CRITERIA ARE BEING ADOPTED?
— Priorities and criteria for services must be developed with professional groups (para 163).

WHAT SKILLS ARE REQUIRED?
— Reviews and adjustments to skill mixes may be necessary. These should be done on the basis of needs assessments, not a cost-cutting exercise (paras 164-166).

— Staff should be adequately trained and updated, especially for child health surveillance tests such as sight and hearing (para 167).

WHAT INFORMATION IS REQUIRED?
— Management information is required, e.g. details of clinic usage, coverage and referral rates of child health surveillance, referrals above specific ages for some conditions. Results should be fed back to practitioners (para 168).

HOW SHOULD THE SERVICE BE ORGANISED?
— A consultant community paediatrician can bring benefits of increased status and drive for quality and evaluation (para 169).

— Organisation of health visiting should take needs of local population into account in order to be cost effective (paras 170-172).

AN AGENDA FOR SOCIAL SERVICES FOR CHILDREN
REVIEWING SERVICES AND COSTS
— Services should be reviewed where this has not yet been done. Quality of provision and the needs of the children supported by social services should not be overlooked in the reviews (para 177).

REVIEWING FIELD SOCIAL WORK PRACTICE AND ORGANISATION
— A review of field social work practice and organisation should be included in any review of services. Amongst issues examined should be: workload management and supervision, spread of resources between teams, response to child protection referrals, time available for non-crisis work, attitudes to 'children in need' (para 179).

REVIEWING RESIDENTIAL CARE
— A review of the current level and future needs for types of residential care may be useful in releasing resources for service developments and improved staffing (paras 180-183).

SETTING A NEW COURSE IN SOCIAL SERVICES
IMPROVING INFORMATION SYSTEMS
— Senior management must have a clear vision of what services are to achieve. Staff at all levels must be equally clear about expected operational and case level outcomes (para 186).

— Information must be collected, analysed and fed back to staff (para 186).

— The experiences and careers of individual children and families must be captured in management information. Financial information must be capable of costing packages of care (para 188).

FIELD SOCIAL WORK
The Role of the Field Social Worker
— Increased specialism within children's social work may well be necessary (paras 189-190).

Sharpening Procedures for Assessments and Care Planning
— Clearer guidance and procedures for assessments and care planning are required (paras 191-192).

Making Better Use of Staff Through Workload Management
— Workload management systems are required which are consistent, prioritise work, take account of skills and provide feedback (para 193).

— Quality of social work practice must also be monitored (para 193).

CHILDREN LOOKED AFTER
Improving the Management of Services
— Residential and foster care should be viewed on a continuum of service options (para 194).

— Important features of an effective fostering service include good support and training of foster carers, and a ceiling on the number of carers supported by a foster care worker (paras 195-196).

— Fostering and adoption should be managed as a service with specialist officers (para 197).

— Residential care should have clear aims and objectives and criteria for referral (para 198).

— Staffing must be appropriate for the homes. Training and status need improving. Residential care staff have skills which can also be valuable in care planning (para 199).

— Residential care staff need supporting. Psychologists may be useful (para 199).

— Admission arrangements to residential care must have explicit terms of reference for gatekeeping panels, involve carers as well as field social workers, and integral arrangements for emergency placements (para 200).

— Social services and education departments need to accept joint responsibility for the problem of disrupted education of children looked after and work together to find solutions (para 201).

Helping Young People Leave Care at Age 16+

— Clear structures, processes and purposes are important with good inter-agency liaison especially between social services, education and housing authorities (paras 202-204).

— A separate structure for supporting young people who have left care may be helpful (para 205).

Appendix 1

Reviewing Residential Care (para 181)

1. The calculations are based on the mix of care exhibited by the nine authorities which had the top rates of fostering in England (excluding authorities that have removed their residential provision completely) according to DoH key indicators. 6 authorities were counties, and 3 metropolitan authorities. The average mix of accommodation for these authorities in 1991/92 was:

    Residential care – 11% Foster care – 71%

    Charge and control – 6% Other – 11%

2. The figure of 11% for residential care was taken as a conservative lower target for the extent of residential provision required.

3. The figure of 11% was applied to all LAs currently above this figure, and the number of places reduction required to reach this level was calculated (DoH indicators IC19 and IC98). The net saving by this reduction was calculated by multiplying the number of places by the weekly unit cost (*52). This is based on the assumption that resources could be released on a marginal (place by place) basis. However, it is recognised that resource savings are only likely to be released if whole establishments can be closed or 'spot purchased' places can be reduced.

4. This savings figure was tempered by a calculation of the additional costs required to support foster care. It is assumed that foster care is the main alternative form of care, although it is accepted that this is not the only option. However, high quality foster care is likely to be the most expensive alternative to residential care. Additional fostering costs were assumed to be as follows:

    Fostering payments – assumed to be £110 per week (the average rate paid in the reference authorities)

    Additional support – assumed to be £1300 per child per year.

5. Additional support – This assumption is based on the cost (including overheads) of a fostering support worker of being around £26,000 per annum, with a reasonable caseload for such a worker being around 20 carers (including additional recruitment work). This is based on published research and on the cost of fostering support in authorities visited.

6. The final estimate of potential financial savings to be released from residential care is a long term estimate. Obviously, this will depend on a managed programme of closure of establishments. Potential for savings will vary widely across authorities, as the extent to which this rationalisation has already occurred varies widely.

Appendix 2

Thanks are due for the advice and guidance of the following who were members of the external advisory group to the project.

John Butler   Professor, Centre for Health Service Studies, University of Kent at Canterbury

Allan Colver   Consultant Community Paediatrician, Northumberland DHA

Carolyn Hey   Deputy Chief Inspector, Social Services Inspectorate, Department of Health

Roy Parker   Professor of Social Policy and Planning, University of Bristol

Chris Perry   Director of Social Services, South Glamorgan County Council

John Rea Price   Director, National Children's Bureau

Ron Spencer   Chief Executive, Cornwall and Isles of Scilly DHA and FHSA

Sheila Shribman   Consultant Community Paediatrician, Northampton General Hospital

Barbara Stilwell   Lecturer, Institute of Advanced Nurse Education, Royal College of Nursing

Norman Tutt   Social Information Systems (former Director of Social Services, Leeds City Council)

Ian White   Director of Social Services, Oxfordshire County Council

✳ ✳ ✳

Special thanks are also due to:

David Hall, Professor of Community Paediatrics, Sheffield Children's Hospital who gave the project team considerable extra advice and guidance in the preparation of the report and the audit guide; and Dr Barry McCormick, Director of the Children's Hearing Assessment Centre, General Hospital Nottingham who gave additional advice to the project team on hearing impairment in young children.

Glossary of Terms

Accreditation
GPs for child health surveillance – FHSAs are required to 'accredit' as competent GPs who wish to receive additional payments under General Medical Services for the provision of child health surveillance services.

Care managers
Person responsible for the co-ordination of services for an individual who has complex needs.

Care plans
Good child care suggests that all children for whom the social services department is providing specific services, should have a child care plan which will describe the programme of services and intended outcomes desired from the services provided.

Child Development Centre (CDC)
A centre which brings together a multi-disciplinary team to assess the needs of and plan services for children with disabilities or other developmental problems.

Children's service plans
Documents to be produced by Social Services Departments, detailing plans for services for children.

Clinical Medical Officers (CMOs)
Career grade community doctors, who often have additional experience in child health.

Community Child Health Services (CCHS)
A wide range of health services, normally provided in the community, aimed to promote the health of children and protect them from disease. These services may be provided by acute or community units, or in a primary care setting by GPs, or by some combination of these.

Community Home
Children's residential home which may be run by the local authority, or the private or voluntary sector.

Developmental surveillance
Programme of checks or observations to ensure that a child is developing normally. Usually carried out by health visitors and either General Practitioners or Clinical Medical Officers.

Family centres
A number of models are available. The Children Act requires local authorities to provide family centres as part of their range of provision. They may be therapeutic, providing highly skilled interventions, or they may be a community based/self help models of provision. Their unique feature is that they work with children and families, unlike nursery or other day care provision.

Family Health Services Authorities (FHSAs)
Authorities which have responsibility for the commissioning and management of family health services. The commissioning role encompasses needs assessment and performance review: the provider role includes a wider responsibility for enhancing value for money in family health services, as well as the pay and rations functions that were the remit of the predecessor authorities - Family Practitioner Committees.

Family support	Any activity or facility provided either by statutory agencies or by community groups or individuals, aimed to provide advice and support to parents to help them in bringing up their children.
GP fundholders	General Practitioners who have elected to hold their own budgets for certain key elements of service.
Health Visitors	Nurses (who usually also have a midwifery training) who have undertaken a year's additional training to specialise with working in the community, with a broader public health / health promotion role. They nominally work with all client groups, although in practice the vast majority of their time is spent working with families who have children aged 0 to 5.
Homestart	A voluntary sector programme using volunteer mothers with some extra training to befriend other, vulnerable mothers to offer help and support.
Leaving care	Local authorities have increased responsibilities under the Children Act to provide advice and support to young people who have been in their care ('looked after') up to the age of 21 if necessary.
Looked after	Children Act term for children for whom the local authority is providing accommodation or care.
Need	Children in need – terms formalised in the Children Act 1989 to include a child who is 'unlikely to achieve or maintain, or to have the opportunity of achieving or maintaining, a reasonable standard of health or development without the provision of services ... by the local authority; his health or development is likely to be significantly impaired or further impaired without the provision for him of such services; or he is disabled'.
Newpin	A volunteer befriending scheme, intended to help support vulnerable or needy parents, mainly through peer support but with some professional advice.
Parenting skills	Skills required by parents to enable them to bring up their children to a reasonable standard of health and development.
Peer support	The provision of help and support by individuals in the local community rather than by professional intervention.
Profiles	Community or caseload profiles produced by GPs and community nurses (health visitors and school nurses) to assist with the assessment of health needs in the community. They will include information on health status and mortality as well as broader indicators of health risks and services availability.
Public health functions	In this context the responsibility of community health staff, such as health visitors, to retain an oversight of the health needs of the community as a whole (e.g. accident rates, prevalence of health damaging lifestyles).
Register - child protection	Local Authorities are required to maintain registers of children who are at risk of 'significant harm'.

Respite care	The provision of short breaks (either day care, foster care or residential care) for families of children (currently provided largely for children who have disabilities) where there may be high levels of stress.
School Health Service	Services provided to ensure that the education of children is not jeopardised by poor health. These services may be provided by Clinical Medical Officers or General Practitioners, and School nurses. The school health service does not provide treatment services, but will offer health promotion, surveillance and immunisation, as well as more specialist functions such as supporting children with disabilities in school.
Sensori-neural hearing loss/deafness	Hearing loss resulting from damage to the cochlear structures and nerve parts. They may be congenital or acquired.
Surveillance	An unsolicited series of tests or observations designed to oversee physical growth and monitor development. The provision of child health surveillance also offers the opportunity to discuss broader health issues and concerns.
Workload management	Systems developed in social services which classify the work (usually of social workers) into a number of broad categories with appropriate weightings for likely levels of effort required. Such systems provide important management information for social services managers.

References

1. NHS and Community Care Act 1990. London, HMSO.

2. Department of Health. General Practice in the NHS – 1990 Contract. 1989, London, HMSO.

3. Children Act 1989, London, HMSO.

4. Convention on the rights of the child adopted by the general assembly of the United Nations on 20 November 1989. London, HMSO, Cm 1976.

5. The Health of the Nation: a strategy for health for England and Wales. 1992, London, HMSO, Cm 1986.

6. Welsh Office, NHS Directorate. Protocal for Investment in Health Gain, Maternal and Early Child Health. Welsh Health Planning Forum, August 1991.

7. Audit Commission. Children first: a study of hospital services. 1993, London, HMSO.

8. Audit Commission, getting in on the Act: Provision for pupils with special educational needs – the national picture. London, HMSO 1992.

9. Benzeval M and Judge K. Deprivation and poor health in childhood: prospects for prevention pp 291 to 324. In Otto H and Flösser G (eds) How to organise prevention – political, organisational and professional challenges to social services. 1992, Berlin, Walter de Giuytel.

10. Woodroffe C et al. Children, teenagers and health – the key data. 1993, Buckingham, Open University Press.

11. Arblaster L, Murray H, Health, housing and social policy: homes for wealth or health? 1993, Socialist Health Association.

12. King's Fund Institute, unpublished analysis of data from the survey of Londoners' Living Standards 1986.

13. Department of Health, Patterns and outcomes in child placements: messages from current research and their implications. 1991, London, HMSO.

14. NHS Management Executive. Child health surveillance – a recommended core programme. HSG (92) 19, London, Department of Health. Also Welsh Office, Welsh Health Circular 92 (54).

15. Hall DMB (ed), Health for all children 2nd edition, Oxford Medical Publications, 1991.

16. Wyke S, Hewison J. Child health matters. Buckingham, Open University Press, 1991.

17. Children Act report 1992. Presented by the Secretaries of State for Health and for Wales by command of Her Majesty. Department of Health. Cm 2144. London, HMSO.

18. Tunstill J. Local Authority policies on children in need. Chapter 9 in Gibbons J (ed) The Children Act 1989 and Family Support. 1992, Department of Health and HMSO.

19. Nursing by Numbers? Setting staffing levels for district nursing and health visiting services. York, Social Policy Research Unit, York University 1992.

20. Butler N and Golding J (eds): From birth to five: a study of the behaviour of a national cohort. 1986, Pergamon, Oxford.

21. Smith T. Family centres and bringing up your children. To be published by HMSO.

22. Gibbons J et al, University of East Anglia. Unpublished research.

23. Home Office, Department of Health, Department of Education and Science, Welsh Office.Working together under the Children Act 1989. 1991, London, HMSO.

24. Butler J, Child Health Surveillance in Primary Care. Department of Health London, HMSO, 1989.

25. Parker R et al (eds). Assessing outcomes in child care: the report of an independent working party established by the Department of Health. 1991, London, HMSO.

26. Staffordshire County Council. The Pindown Experience and the Protection of Children: the report of the Staffordshire Childcare inquiry 1990. 1991, Staffordshire County Council.

27. Bebbington A, Miles J, Children entering care: a need indicator for in care services for children. May 1988 Discussion paper 574/2. PSSRU, University of Kent at Canterbury.

28. Welsh Health Planning Forum. Health and Social gain for children: guidance to inform local strategies for health. August 1993, Cardiff.

29. Nicoll A, Mann S, Mann N, Vyas H. The child health clinic: results of a new strategy of community care in a deprived area. The Lancet, 15 March 1986.

30. Morgan M, Reynolds A, Morris R, Allsop M, Rona R. Who uses child health clinics and why: a study of a deprived inner city district. Health Visitor, August 1989.

31. British Paediatric Association. Health Services for School Age Children : consultation report of a joint working party. December 1993.

32. British Paediatric Association. Outcome Measures in child health. 1992.

33. British Medical Association and NHS Management Executive. Report of the joint working party on medical services for children. November 1992. London, BMA.

34. Jarvis S, Tamhne R, Thompson L, Francis P, Anderson J, Colver A. Pre-school vision screening. Archives of Disease in Childhood 1990, 65, 288-94.

35. Colver AF. Evaluation of surveillance for pre-school children. MD Thesis. 1992, University of Newcastle upon Tyne.

36. Neighbourhood Nursing – a focus for care (The Cumberledge report). London, HMSO, 1986.

37. Department of Health, New world new opportunities: nursing in primary health care March 1993.

38. Department of Health. Choosing with care: the report of the Committee of Inquiry into the selection, development and management of staff in children's homes. 1992, London, HMSO.

Index

References are to paragraph numbers

A

Accidents	7, 22
Adolescents	100
social work	90
specialisation	190
Adoption, management	197
Adoption officers	97
Alternative services	131
Area child protection committees (ACPCs)	41, 132
Audiology service	83
Audit Commission	11, 44

B

Behavioural problems	17, 22, 124
Block contracts	49, 146
British Paediatric Association	155, 159, 169
Budgets	59, 129

C

Care managers	139
Care planning	191, 192
Census data	112
Child abuse	23, 34, 51, 125
Child care, out-of-hours help-line	117
Child development centres (CDCs)	34, 75, 121, 137
Child health clinics	89, 122
health commissioners' agenda	147-150
Child health service organisation	169-172
Child protection	23, 51, 58, 63, 179
assessment procedures	191
collaboration on	64
inter-agency working and co-operation	132-133
management information	133
monitoring	188
social workers' response to referrals	179
Child protection register	37

Children Act 1989	
	3, 5, 8, 10, 40, 59, 72, 90, 100, 129, 133, 173, 178
Children Act Report 1992	44
Children in care	36
Children in need	10
social workers' attitudes to	179
Children 'looked after'	92-100, 194-206
education of	94, 201
proportion not at school	94, 95
Children, Teenagers and Health	16
Children's service plan	110
Clinical medical officers (CMOs)	165
Community child health services:	
commissioning	49
organisation	169-172
Community nurse development unit	126
Computerised information systems	82
Confidence	125
Consultant community paediatrician	169
Co-ordination of services	5, 8, 10, 64, 108, 139
disability support	71, 75, 78
Costs, review	176
Counselling	56, 120
Criminal Justice Act 1991	173
Crisis interventions	48
Criteria, health providers' agenda	163
Cumberledge Report	170
'Customer reception' teams	130

D

Data collection and management systems	89
Day care for under fives	29
Delinquency	22
Demographic information	111
Depression	125
Disability support	24, 51, 65-78, 134-141
care co-ordination	139
co-ordination of services	71, 75, 78
education	77
family centres	68

GPs in   70, 136

   information and advice   69

   joint assessment   137

   joint policies, strategies and operational
      arrangements between agencies   140

   nurseries   68

   parents' assessment of   73

   parents' role   135

   partnership with parents   69

   provision of special aids and equipment 74

   registers   72

   school role   138

   specialisation   190

   survey   67

Diversion model   130

Diversion schemes   128, 131

Divorce   17

E

Education

   alternative   95

   children 'looked after'   94, 201

   children with special needs   11

   disability support   77

Education Act 1993   138

Environmental factors   18

Evaluation, health commissioners' agenda   157-159

F

Family centres   56, 60, 120, 123

   disability support   68

Family health services authorities (FHSAs)
                                                          31, 80, 149, 150

Family relationships   124

Family structure   17

Family support   22, 51, 52, 55

   amount and type required   127

   Case Studies   124

   co-ordination through family centres   124

   expenditure   29

   joint planning and co-ordination   116-131

   local projects   126

   non-professional   61

   outcomes from   60

   professional   61

   provision of   61

'targeted' families   57

Financial information   188

Fostering   23, 28, 36, 92, 97, 181

   costs   125

   management   194, 195-197

Fostering officers   97

G

Getting in on the Act   11

GP clinics, standards of   150

GP contract   31

GP fundholders   85-87

   health commissioners' agenda   151

GP practices   161, 169-172

GPs

   accreditation   84, 149

   collaboration with   89

   in disability support   70, 136

   involvement of   8

H

Health commissioners' agenda   142-159

   child health clinics   147-150

   evaluation   157-159

   GP fundholders   151

   health education   156

   health promotion   156

   health surveillance   145-146

   health visiting   152

   immunisation   145-146

   information   157-159

   monitoring   157-159

   school health service   130-156

   school nurse   153, 154

Health education, health commissioners' agenda   156

Health for All Children   30, 79, 145

Health improvement targets   6

Health of the Nation   6, 143

Health promotion   55

   health commissioners' agenda   156

Health providers' agenda   160-172

   criteria   163

   information systems   168

   priorities   163

   skills requirements   164-167

Health surveillance

health commissioners' agenda   145-146

    school age children   154

Health surveillance programme   30, 31, 79, 80, 82

Health visiting/visitors   31, 33, 49, 50, 53, 162, 166

    activities of   54, 55, 56

    'attached' to GP practices   170

    health commissioners' agenda   152

    'patch-based'   170

    reductions in visiting   119

    routine visiting   118

Hearing loss, screening   83

Hearing tests   150

Help-line   117

Home visits   53

'Homestart'   61

Hospital services   11

Housing conditions   18

I

Immunisation   7, 31, 51, 80, 81, 84

    health commissioners' agenda   145-146

Infant mortality   17

Information systems   93

    computerised   82

health commissioners' agenda   157-159

health providers' agenda   168

    improvements in   187-188

Inter-agency approach   41, 72

J

Joint partnerships   108-141

K

Key requirements   10

L

Local authorities   3, 5, 9, 19

    responsibilities of   26

Londoners' health and lifestyle survey   19

M

Management information   188

    child protection   133

Material circumstances   16

Maternal and Early Child Health_   6

Monitoring

    child protection   188

    health commissioners' agenda   157-159

    residential care   198

Multi-agency approach   113, 131

Multi-purpose centres   122

N

Needs assessment   46, 47, 49, 111, 174, 192

    health providers' agenda   161-162

Needs identification   102, 109, 112

Neglect   23

NHS and Community Care Act 1990   8, 10, 90, 143

Nurseries   123

    disability support   68

Nursery nurses   56, 166

Nursery places   58

P

Parenting skills   21, 56

Parents

    material circumstances   16

    partnership with agencies   10, 104, 105

    responsibility   1, 2

    role of   21, 114, 135

    under stress   125

Partnership between agencies and with

    parents   10, 104, 105

Personal circumstances   15

Physiotherapists   76

Pindown experience and the protection of children   99

Population profiles   54

Priorities, health providers' agenda   163

Proactive services   48, 128

Protocol for Investment in Health Gain   6

R

Residential care   23, 28, 36, 92, 94

    admissions arrangements   200

    costs and cost savings   182

    gate keeping panels to approve admissions   96

    management   194, 198

    monitoring   198

    review   180-185

    role of   98

    staffing levels   99, 199

support force   180

Risk indicators   45, 92, 111

Road deaths   18

S

School age children, health surveillance   154

School entry medical examination   154

School exclusions   11

School health service   34, 88

    health commissioners' agenda   130-156

    staffing of   153

School medical officers   88

School nurses   88, 162, 166

    health commissioners' agenda   153, 154

School role in disability support   138

SCMO   165

Screening tests   167

    hearing loss   83

Self-esteem   125

Sensory stimulation   121

Service provision

content and delivery   20, 32

    defining needs and priorities   43

    formulating strategy   40

    joint activities   40

    patterns of   27, 36, 37

    problems of   39-106

Sight tests   150

Skills requirements, health providers' agenda   164-167

Social services

    agenda for children   173-206

    cost effectiveness   184

    costs review   176

    new strategies   48

    responsibilities of   25, 128

    review   175

    revision of   186

    short and long-term outcomes   92

Social work(ers)   68, 90

    and Children Act   178

    and gatekeeping panels   96

    attitude(s) to 'children in need'   179

    field role   189

    lack of available time   179

    practice and organisation review   177

    research on outcomes   93

    response to 'child protection' referrals   179

    role of   90, 91

    specialisation   189, 190

    spread of resources   179

    supervision   179

    workload management   91, 179, 193

Special education   138

Special schools   77

Spending patterns   27, 28

Staffing levels and population needs   50

State intervention   8

State role   1, 2

U

Underdevelopment   22

Underprivileged area (UPA) score   50

United Nations Convention on the Rights of the Child   2

V

Voluntary agencies   61, 120

W

Weighted workload management schemes   91

Welsh Office   143

Welsh Planning Forum   113

Working Together   64

Y

York Social Policy Research Unit   50

Young adults   26

Young people leaving care   100, 202-205